WE REMEMBER

THE COMING OF THE WHITE MAN

SPECIAL EDITION

In recognition of the
100th Anniversary
of the Signing of Treaty 11

COMPANION DVD INCLUDES

We Remember the Coming of the White Man
Directed by Raymond Yakeleya, 1978
and
We Remember the Coming of the White Man
Director's commentary by Raymond Yakeleya. (55 minutes)
Remastered and produced in 2020.

Also available on Vimeo.
Remastered video (55 min.) – *https://vimeo.com/396055529*
Director's commentary (55 min.) – *https://vimeo.com/396074132*
Password: remember2020

Carry-on-Song. Painting by Antoine Mountain.

WE REMEMBER

THE COMING OF THE WHITE MAN

SPECIAL EDITION

In recognition *of the*

100th Anniversary

of the Signing of Treaty 11

Editors: Sarah Stewart and Raymond Yakeleya
Authors: Walter Blondin, Raymond Yakeleya,
Sarah Stewart, Colette Poitras
Leanne Goose, Antoine Mountain,
George Blondin and Dene Elders

DURVILE & UpRoute Books
Calgary, Alberta, Canada

DURVILE & UpRoute Books

UpRoute Imprint of Durvile Publications Ltd.
Calgary, Alberta, Canada
www.durvile.com

Library and Archives Cataloguing in Publications Data
We Remember the Coming of the White Man
Special Edition in Recognition of the 100th Anniversary of the Signing of Treaty 11

Stewart, Sarah; Editor | Yakeleya, Raymond; Editor

Yakeleya, Elizabeth; Simon, Sarah; Blondin, George; Yakeleya, Raymond;
Goose, Leanne; Mountain, Antoine *et al*; Authors
Blondin, Walter; Foreword | Poitras, Colette; Afterword
Artwork and Illustration | Mountain, Antoine; Schefter, Ruth; Demarais, Deborah
Gwich'in translation; Jerome, Sarah; Ross, Bella
1. Dene People | 2. First Nations | 3. Indigenous | 4. Treaty 11 | 5. Reconciliation

[The UpRoute "Spirit of Nature" Series]
Issued in print and electronic formats
ISBN: 978-1-988824-63-5 (print pbk + DVD); 978-1-988824-75-8 (e-pub)
978-1-988824-74-1 (audiobook)

Cover image, Chief Zaul Blondin of the Sahtù Dene, National Museums of Canada collection.
Elizabeth Yakeleya's poem *Nan Kak* (My Land) was previously published in
Vistas of the West: Poems and Visuals of Nature. Published by Durvile & UpRoute Books, 2019.
Antoine Mountain's story was previously published in *From Bear Mountain*
by Brindle & Glass, an imprint of Touchwood Editions, 2019. Reprinted with permission.
George Blondin's stories were previously published in *When the World was New,*
Outcrop Northern Publishers, 1990.
Reprinted with permission by Ted Blondin and Violet Camsell-Blondin, literary estate executors.

Jacket and book design, Austin Andrews and Lorene Shyba.

We Remember the Coming of the White Man film on DVD included with this book was
remastered by Lorene Shyba from Raymond Yakeleya's 1978 film *We Remember.*

Durvile Publications would like to acknowledge the financial support of
the Government of Canada through Canadian Heritage Canada Book Fund
and the Government of Alberta, Alberta Media Fund.
Sarah Stewart wishes to thank The Canada Council for support, while compiling and editing.

Canada Alberta Government

Printed in Canada. Special Edition, second printing. 2021.

Dedication

This book is dedicated to the memory
of our Dene Elders.

As publisher, authors, and editors,
we also dedicate the book to
future writers and storytellers.
As a collective, we are donating our
publication royalties to establish a prize for emerging
Indigenous writers and storytellers from the North.

"Through this initiative we will continue to find ways to respect each other, learn from each other, and work together to tell the histories of our People."

— Raymond Yakeleya

Contents

Contents

Marie and Joseph Blondin, parents of Walter Blondin, aunt and uncle of Raymond Yakeleya, smoking caribou meat.

Photo: Courtesy of Walter Blondin

Preface

Raymond Yakeleya

THE FIRST EDITION of this book, *We Remember the Coming of the White Man* sold out very quickly, and speaking on behalf of the publisher and editors, this has made us all very happy. This demonstrates a strong and growing interest in the history of the Dene People.

Most of the copies from the first edition were sold directly to people in the North and, as well, through independent bookstores, notably The Yellowknife Book Cellar. The book received acclaim in many newspapers and media including CBC, *The Rocky Mountain Outlook,* Cabin Radio, and *BC Bookworld.* We were also happy to learn that many libraries throughout Canada and the USA purchased the book for their local readers. This cannot help but expand knowledge about the Dene People and, notably, Treaty 11's dubious distinction in Canada's history.

With this Special Edition, we are now in a position to expand our opinions about the signing of Treaty 11, which took place one hundred years ago in 1921. At the beginning of this book Walter Blondin and Sarah Stewart bring clarity to the history and fallout of the Treaty, but one thing I wish to emphasize is that it is important to know that Treaty 11 was initiated because of the oil contained in Norman Wells on the traditional lands of my family, the Blondin family.

When our Dene People signed Treaty 11 in 1921, there had been no negotiation because the Treaty translators were not able to translate the actual language used in the document. There was not enough time either for our People to consult with each other. Our Dene People were given a list that had been written up by bureaucrats declaring the demands of Treaty 11. They dictated to the Dene, "This is what we want. You have to agree, and sign it." We did not know what these papers contained.

In the entire history of our People, we had never come across anything like that before. The government parties would stop in towns and villages along the Mackenzie River for one or two days and demand a signature. How can they demand something from People who cannot understand? That's a crime. I have often said that Treaty 11 does not meet the threshold of being legal. In other words, when we make a treaty, it should be that you understand, I understand, and we agree. In this case, the Dene did not understand.

It was only through the urging of the Roman Catholic bishop in my hometown of Fort Norman, *(Tulita),* that the People signed the Treaty because they had faith in the Roman Catholic Church. I remember my grandfather saying that Bishop Breynat, who was the bishop of the Mackenzie diocese, worked for God and did not lie, steal, or cheat. Belief was that he had to be a completely honest man and so we put our faith in him. It turned out not to be that way. It was all about money and we feel the Catholic Church was in the pocketbook of the government and the Dene were their last concern.

I feel we should challenge Treaty 11 because there are many parts of it that are despicable. We still do not understand Treaty 11 and I think we have to look at it again from the Dene perspective. We are bound by that Treaty and we gave our word. We need to go through the Treaty point by point by point and see where we are at a hundred years later.

That all said there was some benefit of education that came with the Treaty and some health care but overall I have very little to praise. It was obvious the white man was not going to learn Dene so our People were trained in the English language. There was medical care, but there were also many diseases introduced like tuberculosis, measles, polio, and of course, the Spanish flu. Our People had no antibodies to fight these new sicknesses. When I made the film *We Remember* with Bill Stewart, which is included with this book, we found out that the Department of Indian Affairs cut back funding for medicines for Indigenous People. So rather than be a good partner and provide medical care, people died. The government was meant to be a partner who had concern for us but they didn't really give a damn for us. We could not trust them.

The Department of Indian Affairs was also responsible for a lot of the other suffering our People went through, like the Residential School system and the Sixties Scoop. Their idea was to keep us just smart enough to be dumb. Thoughts were, "Don't train the Indian kids much more than grade 3 because they are going to compete with the white man immigrant settlers coming in for jobs."

The Monument Project

WE ARE CURRENTLY GATHERING STRENGTH with other First Nations groups to create an Indigenous monument project for Parliament Hill in Ottawa. As a bit of background, I was part of a delegation from Alberta a number of years ago, when Brian Mulroney was Prime Minister. Native artists were called to Ottawa to help the Government develop policy on how to deliver funding. We came to Ottawa from all across the country — Nunavut, the west coast, prairies, mountains, and the east coast — and we spent a week in meetings and conferences, making many new friends.

On my last day in Ottawa, I went to Parliament Hill and walked around because I knew there were statues that I wanted to see. I was shocked to see there was no representation from First Nations People, even though this is our land. There was nothing and nobody.

As I continued walking around, I saw all these white people being glorified through statues and monuments on Parliament grounds. I imagine some of them were really fine people but the ones I would kick off are the Famous Five Women and Sir John A. MacDonald.

The Famous Five Women from Alberta were Louise McKinney, Nellie McClung, Henrietta Muir Edwards, Irene Parlby, and Emily Murphy. In their time in the 1920s, they knew it was wrong to deny women rights on the grounds that they were women, but they didn't fight for Native women, Black women, or Chinese women. I admired that they fought to have women recognized as people but they only fought for white women. The way I took it is that as white women, they felt they were a little better than other women, which really incensed me because they were showing off their arrogance and prejudice. The Famous Five also supported laws that led to the forced sterilization of women, a great number of whom were Native women.

Looking at early Canadian leaders like John A. MacDonald and Duncan Campbell Scott, it is clear to see they were racist toward the First Nations. They did not deal honestly or openly with our People and that was their first mistake — they were pulling a fast one and stealing from us. One Dene Elder told me, "We've never been to school, but we know how to count our money." He was basically saying that even though we don't speak the same language, we know what's going on. We know a lie when we see it.

I started thinking about how we need a statue that would recognize all Native People of Canada — the First Nations, the Inuit, the Métis — because this is our land and we are still not represented. It was during this time I started writing the proposal that became the "Beothuk: First People Monument of Canada," a monument that recognizes all the hard times our People have gone through as they were being cheated and their lands were being stolen.

This proposed monument would be dedicated to the memory of the Beothuk People, who were a First Nations People from Newfoundland. They had bounties put on their heads and were hunted by British colonizers, becoming extinct in 1829. It is hard to believe, but Beothuk People are no more. If this monument becomes a reality on Parliament Hill, as they go in to make laws, Members of Parliament could look at this First Nations monument and think, "We are here to make laws to help people, not to hurt people." I think it is really important for the lawmakers of the future to look at all Canadians in that way. That's what we hope for and that's what we pray for — that after 150 years, we can reset things with our country.

Crimes were committed against our People but we are still here. I want to do something that will honour our People and if we work with our artists and designers, we can make something of great significance. I want to do something so our Native People can go to a monument which will be dedicated to them to create a place they can go as a sanctuary and as a place to pray. Maybe it could even have a sacred fire. This is something that is needed as a way of reconciliation, as a way of healing, and a way of crying and finding forgiveness in our country. There are still atrocities happening to Native People to this day and we need to work on that.

NEW MATERIAL in this Special Edition of *We Remember* also includes "Part III, Stories by the People" — works by the late George Blondin, Leanne Goose, Antoine Mountain, and myself. These stories bring to life the legends and values of Indigenous People of the North that have been seared in our minds, hearts, and souls since the Beginning of Time. The wisdom of these stories was always there, and so it will always be there. We didn't have books, we carry our learnings and knowledge with us.

We have to pass these stories on to the new generation. With books like *We Remember*, we are bringing the Dene knowledge forward, and I encourage other Native People from across the country, from across the world for that matter, to save what you can. We are losing language and culture very quickly worldwide. I am proud that our books and my film work goes into schools to teach new generations. All of our Elders' words move into the future and I am proud of saving what we can.

White government colonists from the time of Treaty 11 thought that because we couldn't speak English or write things down in our language that we knew nothing. They didn't realize that we had our own languages and that we knew our own history. We knew about God, we knew about prehistoric animals from the last ice age. We knew how to survive in cold, cold weather. They thought they could cheat us but we're smart. We are proud of our language and our culture and we want to keep it. We have nothing to be ashamed or shy about. We like the way our good Creator made us and we thank Him every day.

— *Raymond Yakeleya, 2021*

Dene Drum Dance. Antoine Mountain.

The design for this painting follows along how all Indigenous Peoples do things in a clockwise manner, as the Sun appears to do, every day. So, too, we follow an ancient path.
—Antoine

Part I

Reflections

Foreword: Walter Blondin

Sarah Stewart

Raymond Yakeleya

Colette Poitras

Foreword

Walter Blondin

It is my privilege to write the foreword to this special edition of *We Remember the Coming of the White Man,* a book that recognizes the 100th Anniversary of the signing of Treaty 11 in 1921, the last of the numbered treaties. Treaty 11 was made between the British Crown and the Dene. The Crown refers to the legal embodiment of the executive, legislative, and judicial governance of the United Kingdom as personified by the ruling monarch. Treaty 11 was not made with the Canadian Government as such because Canada, as part of the British Empire, did not have any authority to enter into any treaties until the Statute of Westminster was passed in 1932. However, Canada has inherited the obligation to honour all treaties made with First Nations.

We Remember the Coming of the White Man is an important book which tells of the fallout of those unresolved interactions between the Crown and Canada's First Nations, Métis and Inuit. Variations of these stories, preserved in First Nations' oral histories, are heard in Indigenous communities across Canada and tell how the Canadian Government has not lived up to the promises made when the treaties were signed. The disenfranchisement of the Sahtù Dene of Norman Wells is a clear example of what happens when the state ignores its constitutional obligations.

The Blondin Family

My family, the Blondin family, lived for generations in the Norman Wells area in the Sahtù region in the central Northwest Territories. In 1920, Canada's second oldest oilfield, after Oil Springs, Ontario, was found on our traditional lands. This discovery on unsurrendered Dene lands was the single most important event in the history of the Northwest Territories. It set the stage for the signing of Treaty 11 to enable the Crown to establish ownership of the land's resources.

Blondin Family Portrait

Back Row. Jane Etchinelle, Marie Therese Blondin, Joseph Blondin, Morris Mendo. Walter Blondin

Front Row. Betty Blondin, Charles Blondin, Elsie Blondin, Ethel Blondin, Granny Catherine Blondin.

Photo: From the Collection of Walter Blondin

Treaty 11 forever changed the Dene and Métis relationship with the Crown, which still remains unresolved.

We Dene consider our land as sacred and owned by everyone collectively as it provides life. Before the Treaty, families would hunt, fish and trap in certain areas as there were laws between the families that insured harmony and sharing. No one was left behind to face hardships or to starve when disasters such as forest fires devastated the lands. The Dene laws promoted sharing, and this was taken very seriously as failure to follow these laws could lead to war and bloody conflict. People were honest and transparent in dealing with one another, resulting in peaceful and harmonious interactions.

Catherine Blondin

With her husband Zaul Blondin, Catherine adopted eighteen orphans and gave these children a family and a chance in life.

Artist: Frank Baptiste

The lands around Norman Wells were recognized as traditional territory of the Blondin family and our relatives, who were members of the Fort Norman Band. This land was where we hunted, trapped, fished, and survived for many generations before the White Man ever came to the North. On these traditional lands, petroleum oil was a resource that was an open secret as it seeped to the surface near Bosworth Creek. This is where the Blondin family and relatives had their three main log homes, warehouses and gardens. They used oil for their dog sled runners in the spring to make sleds move more easily on the soft snow. Oil also helped us waterproof our canoes. Everyone was welcome to use this substance as it was meant to be shared. The Blondin family had no idea of its economic potential, however they knew it had special strange magical properties. There are family stories of them experimenting with the oil where they would pour some oil into the fire, which would flare up spectacularly.

They knew this was no ordinary liquid. This had been known for many years, long before Alexander Mackenzie made his famous trip down the Mackenzie River and, in his notes, mentioned signs of oil floating on the water near Norman Wells.

Importance of the Oil

Because of the geographic isolation and lack of information and communication with the outside world, my family did not know that their oil was immensely important to the rest of Canada. Oil was, and is, the liquid that powers and lubricates the machines and economy of countries worldwide. The family did not know that countries fought wars, lied, and cheated to control the sources of oil for their benefit. We all know oil was and is one of the most important resources in the world today. Our world runs on oil, for better or for worse.

In 1912, the Blondin family gave oil samples to the Roman Catholic Bishop for evaluation. These samples were shipped out on the Hudson's Bay Company boat to Edmonton for further laboratory testing. Testing that then took place in Pittsburgh, Pennsylvania. However, no report about that was ever received by the Blondin family. In 1914, unknown and uninvited by the family, Dr. Bosworth, a geologist, staked three claims at Bosworth Creek. In 1918 these three claims were bought by Imperial Oil Ltd. In the late summer of 1919, an Imperial Oil drilling rig, crew, and an ox showed up unannounced and uninvited at Bosworth Creek. The crew immediately began occupying the three log homes and using the warehouses of the Blondin family.

That summer the Blondin family were visiting relatives out on the Mackenzie River and Great Bear Lake. In the fall, when the family returned to their homestead, Imperial Oil personnel began to threaten them about using the food sources around Bosworth Creek. They said to the families, "You are not welcome in your homes and your traditional lands and hunting territory." The Imperial Oil personnel also claimed that the oil seepage and my family's style of living were a fire hazard. The Blondin family was forcibly driven out by these strangers. This was the beginning of the dark and hard times for the family. What were the leaders, Elders, women and children to do with winter coming up and no homes to return to? Denying people food goes against all Dene Laws. No food, no life. It must be remembered that the Dene survived on the land and the land provided everything they needed. Elders say, "It was the first time in living memory where the Dene became homeless on their own land."

In the summer of 1920 drilling started, and oil was struck at seven hundred feet. This oil discovery was historically important. It was Canada's first oilfield. All three Blondin family homes and warehouses were now occupied by Imperial Oil drilling staff. After several winters, these homes were torn down and pushed over the riverbank with all the family possessions. This was the first time that homes were destroyed by Imperial Oil.

The second time the homes were torn down was in the 1940s when five homes, built by the Blondin family at the transmitter sites, south of Norman Wells, were destroyed and also pushed over the riverbank. This practice continued well into the 1970s. No apology or compensation was ever received from Imperial Oil. Imperial Oil considered Norman Wells to be "their town—a White Man's town" and the Blondin family and other Dene were not welcome.

In 1920 oil was struck near the current site of Norman Wells.

Photo: Norman Wells Historical Society

My father, Joe Blondin, once said, "Right now, Norman Wells is a white community. The Natives can't even pitch a tent there. I was born and raised there but all I can do is walk the streets. They are choking us little by little."

Chief Zaul Blondin and the Treaty Party

Chief Zaul Blondin, who is on the cover of this book, was the Blondin family leader and signatory as Second Chief for the Fort Norman People in signing Treaty 11 in 1921. He was also a shaman, a spiritual leader, and noted humanitarian. He and his wife, Catherine, adopted eighteen orphans and gave these children a family and a second chance in life. "No one should be left behind," was their belief. Chief Zaul Blondin never expected that his family and relatives would be fighting for their very survival on their own lands.

The Treaty Party talked of Treaty 11 being the "treaty of friendship." However, Treaty 11 became the "treaty for oil ownership." Oil and land surrender were never once mentioned in these talks with the Dene Bands who were signatories to this treaty. It should be noted that the Crown stated that these talks were "negotiations." The Treaty was written in English legalese language that the Dene interpreters could not understand nor interpret, and the people had to rely on what they were promised verbally by Indian Agent, Henry Conroy. The Dene did not know that Conroy was not there to negotiate. The written words of the Treaty could not be altered. Conroy only wanted to obtain signatures and marks from the Dene Leaders to legalize this charade. What the Crown really wanted, and the Dene did not know it, was control of their land and its resources.

When Henry Conroy presented Treaty 11 to the Dene in 1921, no mention was made of the *Migratory Birds Convention Act* that was signed in 1917 among Canada, United States, and Mexico. This international act was passed into law to stop the shooting of ducks, geese, swans and other migratory birds on their annual migration from Mexico to Canada to prevent the white man's exploitation and possible extinction of the birds. Canada's Native People were never consulted and were unaware of this political move eliminating their important food source.

The main concern of the Dene was to have a food source that was not regulated by the Canadian Government by game laws. Our People did hear from Treaty 8 Dene, from the southern Northwest Territories, that shortly after Treaty 8 was signed, game laws and game wardens were in the territory to enforce the new laws. The exclusion of this *Migratory Birds Convention Act* information was critical to the Dene's signing of Treaty 11. The Crown purposely withheld this bit of important information and they were openly deceitful in the important information presented.

Dene Elders say, "Treaty 11 was already written up in legal language that they and their translators could not understand." In a treaty, both sides should clearly understand what is on the table and what is agreed to. No assumptions.

Three Sahtù Chiefs and their wives
Left to Right. Wife of Chief Jimmy Soldat, Chief Jimmy Soldat, Harriet Wright, Chief Albert Wright, Catherine Blondin, Chief Zaul Blondin

Photo: From the Collection of Walter Blondin

Treaties

Treaties were agreements between the European states and countries going back to earlier times and were binding agreements for peace, for alliances and for commerce. First Nations of Canada had something similar. They negotiated issues and conflicts and had a clear understanding with regards to alliances, truces and peace. This was a common and simple approach that worked. Nothing was written. These agreements stayed alive in people's memories and were passed down through stories to every generation, to this day.

There is also a question about signatures and marks on Treaty 11. Chief Julien Yendo, of Wrigley, NWT, said upon seeing his mark on Treaty 11, "That is not my mark, for I was in the bush hunting." This raises the question of fraud.

When Imperial Oil started developing the oilfield and refining the oil at the Norman Wells refinery, they recognized Chief Zaul Blondin and his family's connection to the oilfield by setting a precedent of compensation and giving Zaul Blondin free gas for the rest of his life. This was small comfort for the destruction, prejudice, racism and misery that came to the family. ExxonMobil, now primary owner of Imperial Oil, is one of the largest and wealthiest oil companies in Canada. To date, 276 million barrels of oil have been recovered from the Norman Wells field and it is still producing.

Treaty 11 should not be considered legal as the Dene did not understand the legal language of the Treaty. One hundred years after the fact, the Dene can see the collusion between the British Crown, Imperial Oil and the Roman Catholic Church in the fraud, theft and embezzlement of Dene resources. This book, and the DVD film that comes with it, tell our story, give our oral history. There have been many discussions in private though not in public, bringing out important legal and ethical questions that need to be answered at the highest levels from the Canadian Government. For example: How did Imperial Oil, now majority-owned by the US company ExxonMobile, obtain two-thirds ownership of the Norman Wells field? As mentioned, it is estimated that 276 million barrels of sweet crude oil have been taken from the field.

What was the role of the Roman Catholic Church during Treaty 11 talks in the NWT? It appears to the Dene that the Roman Catholic and Anglican Churches were given total responsibility by the Crown to operate the Residential Schools and have almost total control of the Northern education system as part of the government's policy to destroy the culture of the First Nations people. It also appears that the Roman Catholic Church was the insurance that the Crown needed so that the Dene would sign Treaty 11. The Dene were suspicious of the Crown and its agents' promises and were hesitant to sign Treaty 11. Fort Norman witnesses said that,

"This was the moment when Bishop Breynat told the People that the signing of Treaty 11 was beneficial to them and would help them." It was at that moment that the Dene thought differently, as most Dene were devout Roman Catholics. The Elders said, "The Bishop works for God and he cannot steal, lie or cheat or do anything wrong. So he must be speaking the Truth." It was at this moment that the Dene agreed to sign a legal document that they did not understand and one that the translator could not translate. The Dene had faith in the Bishop's words even though he was deceiving them.

During the treaty talks, was the Crown acting in collusion with Imperial Oil and the Roman Catholic Church? It appears now to the Dene that a deal was struck for ownership and division of the oil resource long before Treaty 11 was signed. Treaty 11 was a charade to legitimize the land grab in the Northwest Territories.

Why did the Crown not protect the Blondin family from the racism and abuses perpetrated on them by Imperial Oil? The Crown had legal responsibility to protect all Dene from these types of illegal actions.

Raymond Yakeleya, formerly from Fort Norman, now Tulita, has told me many harrowing personal and family stories of the mistreatment by Imperial Oil of the Blondin family. Raymond's grandmother, Elizabeth Yakeleya was a member of the Blondin family, as was his Uncle Joe Blondin. One of the significant stories by Elizabeth Yakeleya is the story about her father Francis Blondin. As Raymond describes it,

> My grandfather Francis Blondin had to relocate his family to Fort Norman due to the occupation of their homes by drilling crews at Norman Wells. When Grandpa Francis was killed in an accident stalking logs in Fort Norman this was a result of relocation of his family. Granny Elizabeth and her brother and sister were sent to Fort Providence Residential School. Her mother had no home or means to look after her family. During that winter, Elizabeth's mother passed away leaving her three

> children orphaned with no home or family. As Granny Elizabeth Yakeleya said, 'This was real hard times.'"

Thankfully, the children's uncle, Chief Zaul Blondin and his wife Catherine Blondin, adopted them. In the 1990s, days before they died, Elizabeth Yakeleya and Joe Blondin asked Raymond to record the family stories on film about the criminal treatment, dehumanization, institutional racism and human rights violations by Imperial Oil and the Crown. This task was partly completed by the film We Remember, and now the book, We Remember the Coming of the Whiteman.

Dene Elders are still seeking the truth, a just legal settlement, compensation and an apology to the family and the Dene People of the North. It is my hope that this special edition of We Remember the Coming of the White Man will help Raymond with a promise he made to his Elders before they died that their side of the story would be told. Raymond's vow is that "I will keep my word." He is the one who made this book and the original movie possible. This story, and this book, have been 100 years in the making.

Treaty 11

Sarah Stewart

King George V, who dispatched representatives from the Government of the Dominion of Canada to meet with Dene and Métis Chiefs and People of the Mackenzie Valley.

IT WAS 1921 and news came to the Dene and Métis of the Mackenzie Valley that King George V of the United Kingdom was sending his representatives from the Government of the Dominion of Canada with Treaty 11 for them to sign. The Dene and Métis were told where and when they would all meet during that summer.

Many welcomed the Treaty in theory, viewing it as a coming together in peace with white people, to live in future harmony on the land. The Dene expected to have their inherent traditional and Indigenous rights respected and confirmed by treaty, to be protected from encroachment on their land, from intrusion and competition from white trappers, to have access to medical aid, and for their children to be educated. In the Indigenous world view, a treaty was not what was contained in written words on paper, but rather a spoken negotiation between equals, agreed on in good faith and trust.

Since the coming of white people, there had been many changes to the Dene way of life. European diseases of smallpox, influenza, measles, whooping cough, tuberculosis, to name a few, had decimated Indigenous populations throughout the Americas. Those who survived disease were often left disabled. Traditional healers had no experience in treating these diseases to which Indigenous people had little to no immunity.

White trappers had moved on to Dene land and were trapping out the animals whose numbers were diminishing. Some species were on the verge of extinction. *The Migratory Birds Convention Act,* a law in Canada since 1916, stated that, without a waiver, it was unlawful "to pursue, hunt, take, capture, kill, or sell approximately eight hundred species of birds." This law was passed to protect the migratory bird population decimated by Europeans for commercial gain. In 1917, there were closed seasons on moose and caribou hunting. Neither of these laws noted exceptions for Indigenous people or recognition of their dependence on game for sustaining their way of life.

The teachings of missionaries and missionary schools were eroding the native languages, cultures and traditions. Hand in glove came the Hudson's Bay Company, reinforcing Indigenous Peoples' dependence on guns, ammunition, twine, and essentials such as flour and tea.

The Dene's hopes for the Treaty ran counter to those of the Treaty Party and were nothing like what the Government of Canada had in mind. To them, this was simply a real estate deal. The Indigenous People were to give up title to their land and in return would receive as little as the Government of the Dominion of Canada thought they could get away with. As stated in Treaty 11, the Indigenous People would "surrender and yield up to the Government of the Dominion of Canada, for His Majesty the King and His Successors forever, all their rights, titles, and privileges whatsoever to the lands included within the following limits." This was followed by a detailed map outline of the 950,000 km^2 that were being ceded. The Treaty's purpose was, "To open [the land] for settlement, immigration, trade, travel, mining, lumbering and such other purposes."

Treaty 11 gave great rewards to the Government of Canada; a land rich in oil and gas deposits which would soon yield gold, silver, radium, uranium, tungsten, zinc, lead, and diamonds. Trade in furs also hit a high point in value in 1920 and continued to make many white trappers very rich as they trapped out the animals.

The cost to the government for this abundance was an initial outlay of $44,000 and $25,000 thereafter for annuity payments.

In the prairies, Treaties 1 to 7 had already opened the land for farming, the railroad, for towns and cities. But it took another twenty years for the Government to turn its eyes North. Northern Canada had been deemed not worth the expense or the administrative trouble of further investment because there did not appear to be anything there worth having. That is until Imperial Oil struck oil in Norman Wells in 1920. In the excitement, it was reported that the financial benefit to Canada would be enough to wipe out the national debt.

To make the most of the oil and gas industry, title to the land would have to be in the Government's hands and not in Imperial Oil's pocket. Indigenous People, whose land it was, were never considered equal partners in benefitting from the resource. As Indian Agent Henry Conroy wrote to the Deputy General of Indian Affairs in January 1921, the objective was to have Indigenous people surrender their territory "to avoid complications in the exploitation of oil."

Time was of the essence. Indian Agent Walker wrote in 1897 to the Superintendent General of Indian Affairs that Indigenous people "will be more easily dealt with now than they would be when their country is overrun with prospectors and valuable mines be discovered. They would then place a higher value on their rights." The government department of Indian Affairs was concerned also that, if they delayed, Indigenous groups would learn that promises made at other treaty signings had been broken. What was written in the treaties differed significantly from what was promised.

What was the Government giving in return for so many riches? In the words of the Treaty, the Indigenous People will "be assured of what allowances they are to expect and receive from His Majesty's bounty and benevolence." This bounty and benevolence included ten axes, five hand-saws, five augers, one grindstone with files and whetstones to keep the equipment sharp, per group. Fifty dollars worth of hunting and fishing equipment was allocated to each family but only after the Treaty was signed. Hunting and fishing equipment to the value of $3 was to be provided annually to each family.

It was stressed that there was also a present, a present of money. The chief would receive $32, each Headman $22 and the rest of the people would receive $12 each. Every year thereafter, each chief was to receive $25, each Headman $15 and everyone else $5. There was no allowance for inflation.

Chiefs and headmen would get a new suit of clothing every three years. In addition, the Chief was to receive a silver medal commemorating the Treaty, a flag, and a paper copy of the Treaty.

The government agreed "to pay the salaries of teachers to instruct the children of said Indians in such manner as His Majesty's government may deem advisable."

As regards land use, reserves were to be allotted in proportion to one square mile per family of five, which was flexible depending on family size and could be appropriated anytime the land was required for public works. The Treaty states, "His Majesty the King hereby agrees with the said Indians that they shall have the right to pursue their usual vocations of hunting, trapping and fishing throughout the tract surrendered as heretofore described, subject to such regulations as may from time to time be made by the Government of the Country acting under the authority of His Majesty, and saving and excepting such tracts as may be required or taken up from time to time for settlement, mining, lumbering, trading or other purposes."

On June 21,1921, Henry Conroy, accompanied by a Royal

Canadian Mounted Police Inspector and two Constables, left Edmonton bound for the Mackenzie Valley to have every community sign the Treaty and thus extinguish their land title. Conroy would depend heavily on the support of missionary Bishop Gabriel Breynat, O.M.I., who also joined the Treaty Party.

Earlier in 1921, Conroy and Bishop Breynat had asked the Fisheries Department to guarantee the fishing rights of Indigenous people. The answer was a resounding no and they were informed that they "should be guided by the terms set forth [in the Treaty] and . . . no outside promises should be made by you to the Indians." The Treaty Party had no mandate to negotiate.

The stage was set for a clash of cultures. The provisions provided in the Treaty show ignorance of the ways of the Dene by offering them agricultural implements, adzes or hoes for cultivating crops and grinding stones for wheat, useless to a hunting and gathering culture. The decision-making process inflicted on the Dene echoed the hierarchical structure of British society with one man at the top making decisions for the rest. A chief and up to two counsellors or headmen were asked to speak for everybody. And, of course, there was to be no negotiation, but that soon went by the wayside. As the sole objective for the Treaty Party was to get the paper signed, Conroy gave the appearance of negotiation. He was ready to say whatever was necessary to persuade the Dene to sign. He appeared to be negotiating, though he had no mandate, to made promises that he knew could not be kept, and betrayed the trust they were given by those meeting in good faith.

The role of Bishop Breynat cannot be underestimated. In fact, he did not underestimate it himself and took credit for the Indigenous people signing the Treaty in many communities. The trust placed in him as a man of God by the people convinced them that when the Bishop said that they were not selling their land, then it must be true.

The Treaty Party made its way first to Fort Providence where the people signed on June 27th. Chief Paul Lefoin asked that freedom to hunt, fish, and trap be guaranteed, and Conroy and Bishop Breynat guaranteed it. In his book, *As Long as This Land*

Shall Last: A History of Treaty 8 and Treaty 10, Dene advocate Father Rene Fumoleau, wrote about the negotiations at Fort Providence. The evidence he gathered from Elders shows, "All the witnesses stress the fact that it was only after complete freedom to hunt, to trap, and to fish had been promised to the Indians, that they accepted the Treaty."

The next community was Fort Simpson, where the Treaty was signed on July 11th. At first, the people did not want the Treaty and would not sign it. After three days, Bishop Breynat took his opportunity to persuade Antoine, to sign when the actual chief, who had been chosen, went off to eat.

In Fort Wrigley, the Treaty was signed on July 13th. Julian Yendo, the chief, said he was not signing and did not understand the Treaty. But, in the end, because he trusted Bishop Breynat, he signed for his people.

At Fort Norman, now Tulita, the Treaty was signed on July 15th by Chief Albert Wright and Headman Zaul Blondin. At least one-third of the people were away hunting. As recounted in this book, the Elders in Fort Norman stated that they were sure the money they were offered was in exchange for their land. The Treaty Party said it was not for their land but for signing the Treaty. The promise was given in perpetuity. Where the oil and gas ownership fitted into that was not mentioned.

Fort Good Hope signed on July 21st where it took five days of persuasion. Many people were away from the community, hunting or fishing. At Arctic Red River, the people signed in one day, July 26th.

Conroy went without Bishop Breynat to Fort Macpherson as the Gwich'in were Anglican and the Roman Catholic Bishop held no sway. The people signed on July 28th. Jaby Lalo (also spelled Juby) and Johnny Kikawchik or Kyikavichik (named as Johnny Kaye in this book) signed the Treaty. What the people were promised and what they actually got is recorded in this book.

In the last community of Rae, now Behchoko, almost half of the people were away hunting, but the Treaty was signed on August 22nd. Tlicho Elders, who were present at the signing, told

Father Fumoleau that they were promised annual payments and services, such as medical care, education and old age care.

By September 11, 1921, the Treaty Party was back in Edmonton, its job done. It had changed the lives of 3,400 Dene. The oil and gas companies could move in and anyone else who wanted to take what they could get.

In 1922, Indian Agent Harris went North to administer the terms of Treaty 11. He also supervised the signing of Treaty 11 at Fort Liard which had not been completed the previous year. The report of October 12, 1921, on the signing of Treaty 11 written by Conroy, notes that 65 per cent of people had not been present for the signing in at least three communities: Fort Norman/Tulita (136 people); Fort Good Hope (134 people); and Rae/Behchoko (360 people). In fact, an entire community in the basin of the Mackenzie River in Yukon was also missed. Many Dene continued to come forward to sign the Treaty in 1922 and 1923. They had little choice now as the rest of the community had already signed.

The Years that Followed the Signing

In the years that followed, education and health care were still provided by the churches and this continued until the 1950s. Education had only been provisionally and vaguely offered in the Treaty and only according to what the Government "deemed fit," without regard to the needs of the family or community. As for the land, it was sold.

Disenfranchisement of Indigenous people continued in the following years. They were relentlessly removed from lands all across Canada, subjected to numerous ploys to reduce their numbers and withhold their Indian Status. The grand plan was to totally destroy their culture and assimilate them into white society. The numbered treaties, of which Treaty 11 was the last, were the most important steps in making this happen.

It has taken many years to begin redress: from 1921 to 1992 when the Gwich'in settled their land claim; to 1994 when the Sahtù Dene settled; and to 2003 for the Tlicho Dene. These comprehensive land claim settlements include provisions that enable

Indigenous groups to own land, participate in managing the land and its resources, share in revenue generated from resource development, and to govern themselves.

Treaty 11 was also a vehicle for settling land claims with the Métis who were included only if they were living an Indigenous way of life. The Métis received scrip and a certificate, redeemable for land or money, in exchange for their land rights. Northern Métis family names referred to in historical records are Camsells (sic), Gaudet, Beaulieu, Lafferty, McDonald, Smith, and Firth. At least another 75 Métis families were mentioned as signing the Treaty.

References for this Essay

René Fumoleau, *As Long as this Land Shall Last: A History of Treaty 8 and Treaty 11, 1870–1939* (2004).

Report of the Commissioner for Treaty No. 11 by H.A. Conroy, Commissioner for Treaty No. 11 in the National Archives.

A Historical Interpretation of Treaty 11 by Kenneth S. Coates and William R. Morrison from Indigenous and Northern Affairs, Canada.

Transcript of Treaty 11 and Map of Canada 1921 from Indigenous and Northern Affairs, Canada.

We Remember, the Film

Raymond Yakeleya

ALTHOUGH THE MAIN FOCUS of this Special Edition of *We Remember the Coming of the White Man* has shifted to the events of Treaty 11, knowing about the film on DVD that is included with this book brings meaning to the upcoming stories by our Dene Elders. As was the case with the 2020 edition, this 2021 edition of the book also brings together a remastered version of my 1978 film together with priceless "extra footage" by way of transcriptions of Elders' interviews. The original *We Remember* film was duplicated and re-duplicated so many times through the years that Elders' words became difficult to hear in places, so we cleaned up the soundtrack, added subtitles, and sharpened the video images. There is also a director's commentary so you can hear my comments along the way.

By way of some background to the making of the film in the first place, in the late 1970s, I was working for the National Film Board in Montreal when their first big budget cuts came along and junior jobs got cut, including mine. I was wondering what my next step would be and the next day I got a call from CBC North, asking me if I would come back to Northwest Territories to work on three short films for them and I said, "Yeah, I'm your guy!"

So they flew me to Yellowknife and we started working on the films. The first one was about spring hunting at Jackfish Lake with my uncle, Joe Blondin and CBC was really pleased. They were setting up a national studio at the time because they didn't have a Northern feed into the national system. So when I was there, they looked at my work — I was only 23 at the time — and they asked me if I had any ideas about what they could make. They wanted to start with a real bang because Yukon and NWT were under-represented parts of the country.

My idea was that we could make a film about how our Dene Elders perceived the white man coming into our territory. I told them we have the Hudson's Bay Company reports and the missionary reports and that we always hear from the white man but we don't hear from our People. I explained to them that we have been here for thousands of years and suddenly these strange white people come in with funny ideas to start populating the North. CBC liked my idea because they came to realize that the Dene People had their own perspective and their own stories. I wrote it up by saying, "This is about asking the Elders questions they have never been asked before. They have a bunch of answers but answers will stay there unless we open the door for them. And then they will come through." This was something new to CBC and that's how the film *We Remember* was born and indirectly, how this book was born too.

So I got in touch with the Elders all the way from my hometown Tulita northwards toward Aklavik, amongst the Sahtú Dene and the Gwich'in Dene. Bill Stewart was the editor on the film and a very important collaborator because even though he was from England, he really liked being among the First Nations People. Our cameraman was Bob Charlie from Yukon, and Rory MacVicar from Thunder Bay was the audio guy. I admitted to them all that I was inexperienced as a boss and that I needed their experience to be a good director and they were always ready to help.

We took off down the Mackenzie River and met fabulous Elders who were willing to work with us. The Elders really liked that it was a Dene who was asking the questions because it is our perspective of history. When we got back to review the footage that we shot — we shot it all on 16 mm — Bill said to me, "Raymond, I don't know how we are going to cut this down to a half hour documentary. We're going to have problems because this material is so good." Easily there were fifteen to twenty hours of footage. My answer was, "Let's cut it to an hour and just not tell our bosses. This will be our secret." When it came time for CBC to look at the rough cut, they agreed to find us the money to do it in two half-hour parts instead of just one, and that's how the film was originally made. In the remastered version in this book, we combined the two parts together.

Raymond Yakeleya on location of his We Remember film, with Jim Sittichinli.

Photo: Frame from the film, We Remember, 1978.

If CBC had chosen to do a white man side of the story, we might have heard something like, "Let's do Alexander Mackenzie's journeys of exploration," but that's not the First Nation perspective. What did the Dene really think of Alexander Mackenzie? They didn't think very highly of him. Mackenzie's Dene name translated into "long neck" and they perceived him as being very lazy because he was being paddled around all the time. He didn't work as a Chief would with his people.

Alexander Mackenzie didn't have good things to say about the river that bears his name, in fact he called it "The River of Disappointment" because it wasn't a shortcut to the Pacific Ocean. But to the Dene People, the river was a river of life — a highway that would lead Dene People from town to town to trade with our relatives. It was something special for us and in our language we call it the Dehcho, which means the Great River. Our perspective of the Dehcho was different from Mackenzie's because of its great usefulness. In wintertime we'd drive dog teams along it to visit relatives and friends, and in summer we'd take boats to hunt moose and to fish. The Dehcho has great meaning to us for its fishing places, meeting places, and sacred places.

But the white men did not think like that, they thought, "How can we make money off this?" Dene People are not motivated by that. For us, the value comes from places along the river that are holy places so you go there and make offerings and pray, because our inner spirit needs to be revived and refreshed with a spiritual connection. The white man does not see that in our lands or in other First Nation lands. But we see that.

Something that would have come out much differently if white people had told the story is the discovery of oil. The members of the Blondin family talk about their experiences and how it affected my own family to a great extent. The Blondin central camp family homes were in what became Norman Wells and oil has been oozing out of there for thousands of years. They used the oil to treat the runners on their dogsleds, especially in the spring when the snow was soft, and to seal up canoes to waterproof them. Other Dene would be able to recognize canoes from Norman Wells because of their black bottoms.

The Blondin family would always invite other people to come and use the oil because it was meant for everyone, so they would use it on their boats in the summer and on their sleigh runners so they could travel in wet snow. They didn't know about petroleum at the time but they knew they had something special. They did not know how to read or write because the white man's education system had not got to them yet, but they eventually learned about claims and how you could put a claim to the land.

Dene People realized later that because they were not citizens of Canada, they had no rights — only the white man had rights to the mineral wealth. But the white man only wants wealth, that's what their minds are geared for. They come onto the land and say, "Where's the timber, where's the salmon, where's the gold, where's the oil? Where are the really good lands we can put a farm on?" Our People are not like that. We look for the good hunting territories, where we can find caribou and moose or mountain sheep and things that sustain us.

As my Granny Elizabeth Yakeleya says in her poem at the beginning of this book, our land is sacred to us because the land keeps us alive. Both she and my Uncle Joe Blondin would say, "We come from the land, our language comes from the land, our visions come from the land, everything we are comes from the land. And when we die we go back to the land. The land is alive and that's why we are alive, because of its magic." In our language we call this magic "Ik'ǫ́" and with Ik'ǫ́ we can bring the magic of the land to reality.

First Nations People across North America see the land as a holy and magical place because of Ik'ǫ́ and it is because the land is alive that we are alive. It gives us our songs, stories and prophesies and that's why we have so much love and respect for the land. The land has diamonds, and emeralds and all manner of riches, but these are not our treasures. The holy places are our treasures because they are gifts to our spirit. As Dene, we are never afraid of the Creator. The bible people say you have to fear God. Dene People will say, "We are not afraid of God, we love the Creator. We will go right up and talk to Him."

A while ago, when I was in the mountains with the Shutow Dene we went down river near the Yukon border. It was springtime. The water was really high and pouring into the mountain rivers. We were about to go through a particularly dangerous part of the river called The Elbows, which is a zig zag, cutting through stone. If our mooseskin boat was to hit the rock, it would slice our boat in half. We would have drowned in no time. I was talking to one of my uncles about this. He told me that a long time ago — and even today before beginning a dangerous journey — they would have somebody who could make an out-of-body experience and time-travel into the future, down the river and look on the river to see how bad it would be. They would report to the Chief about rapids or log jams, or other dangers, making travel safe for those setting out.

When my Granny Harriet died, the Elders time-travelled again with her because they wanted to examine her life. This time they went backwards in time, came back and gave a report that she had died without sin. I don't know how they time-travel — I am not

Prophet Ayah from Deline.
Photo: National Museums of Canada

gifted for that, but some of our People are gifted that way.

Some of our People can see the future too, including Ayah, famous prophet of the Dene who is sometimes called 'Nostradamus of the North.' He predicted the explosion of the atomic bomb and the coming of the atomic age. The sad thing is that the uranium used by scientists in New Mexico came from our Dene land near Great Bear Lake. Our material was used at White Sands which was the first atomic bomb explosion and after that at Hiroshima and Nagasaki. Ayah called them all. Our People were gifted with that kind of magic. They prophesised and could look into the future.

Animals, to the Dene People, are like family to us and our first teachers. We revere the animals. For example the wolf taught us to work together. That is the success of the wolf pack. Wolves know how to work together. Even though wolves have distinct personalities, they work together for the survival of the whole group. My Uncle Jeremy has a story where he was paddling on Willow Lake in his small hunting canoe that we call a rat canoe. We use them to hunt muskrat and beaver — they're really fast, sit high in the water and don't make any sound. He liked hunting alone to absorb the energy of nature, but suddenly, on the lake, he heard people talking our language. He turned around a corner and saw a family of wolves — mother, father and their pups. They saw him and turned around to run away. Uncle Jeremy gently said, "Don't run away, I want to paddle up to you, meet you, and have a little rest. Would that be okay with you?" So he spent most of the afternoon talking to them. That was his Ik'ǫ́, his medicine power. The wolf.

Mooseskin Boat, Gravel River.

Photo: Norman Wells Historical Society

Every Dene has an animal as their Ik'ǫ or medicine power. My grandmother Elizabeth Yakeleya was a black bear and my dad was a beaver. As for me, I am the raven Tatsǫ. The animals are the ones who select us when we are born. The white man has guardian angels but Dene medicine power is different because the animals decide. They might say, "Well, now that the Raymond child is born, who is going to work with him and help him for all of his life?" And the raven Tatsǫ says, "I'll help Raymond" — just as the black bear might have said, "Oh, I'll help Granny here."

They all bring something good to you. When we look to the animals, the wolf is good for organizing, the beaver is really good at surviving winter because they have to have food all winter and ration the food. The beaver taught us how to survive all those months when the land is frozen and how to make a home. Every animal has their own medicine and their own values and brings a gift for us. Usually you see an animal in your dream and the animal says, "I'm here to be with you for the rest of your life. I will teach you a song and if you sing that song, my spirit will come to you and help you. You are not alone, I have chosen to be with you."

As I say, my animal is Tatsǫ́ the raven. Amongst the Dene, Tatsǫ́ is the leader of all the living things, even ahead of the People. Tatsǫ́ was made first by the Creator, so he has precedence over everybody. He is an unusual animal because being a leader means being truthful, responsible, and having patience — all the things that Tatsǫ́ didn't want to do. The raven is a mischievous personality and loves fun. I think that he was the wrong guy to be the leader, but in spite of all his mischief, he did good things, like setting laws. If you are ever going to be a friend of any animal, talk to the raven in a good way. He is a very communicative animal and loves to have friends. If you are his friend, he will help you.

Talking about Dene magic, another thing our People can do is change weather. The Frog Clan of the Carrier Dakelh Dene, who live in British Columbia, are famous for that. Frogs are notable for being able to live on the land and live in the water so Carrier Dene use frogs in a ceremony to change weather. I found that out when I was working with the Carriers, their specialty was using frogs to change the weather. I had never heard of that among our People, the Northern Dene.

A man who can change the weather is a very valuable man to have. Among the Northern Dene, for example, if you are hunting moose and you're not having much luck in the winter time, my Uncle Joe Kenney and others like him could create a blizzard storm. Once you create a blizzard storm you make it ideal for moose hunting because swirling winds confuse the moose. (Moose have long ears like radar and can tell what direction something is coming from but if you have whirling winds they cannot tell what direction you are coming from.)

Some of the medicine men can also call animals when People are hungry. There is a legend where a medicine man saw that People in Deline were starving, so he got out his drum and started singing a song. Muskox that were in the region came toward town. People were able to kill some muskox, and that's what saved our People. Medicine men are very important because they have a relationship with animals. When you kill an animal, you have a conversation with it and give it thanks for sharing its body. There are special protocols and ceremonies you have to go through.

Giving thanks for an animal when you kill it is part of Tatsǫ's rules that the animals and Dene People agreed upon. Tatsǫ finalized it by saying, "We all okay with this? Everybody okay? Any dissenters? No? Okay, then we'll go with it." Tatsǫ was brilliant that way.

We had people amongst us who knew plants for healing and they were like our doctors. White people had university doctors but our People were natural healers who could do the same thing as the doctors. Our People could travel with stars at night and our People could communicate with animals. We knew about our sacred sites where special things could happen on the land. So we all pay homage to that and recognize these things as part of the Dene world. When I talk to our medicine people, I know they always strive for us to be in balance with things. It is very important to be in balance with nature.

A MAJOR CONFUSION came to our People with the coming of the Catholic missionaries. I see the coming of the Black Robes as being a very, very dark cloud that descended over our People. All of a sudden you have people from another culture with another way of thinking imposing their laws. We see they did it for money, control, and power. I heard an Elder say to me once that the Christians who followed the Ten Commandments were the same people who broke all of them.

We even see their influence today. They created nothing but trauma for the People, especially the boarding (residential) schools. The first time we ever questioned ourselves was with the coming of the Christians and to me, I think there was something evil that came amongst our People. We are now talking openly about that. The missionaries were quick to pass judgment on our People and were quick to say our ways were the ways of the devil, or the ways of something not good. And we watched them, and said, "Who are these people throwing mud at us?" Now we see they are being charged with pedophilia and other crimes. They'd walk around masquerading as something good when all along there was a lot of evil.

I have to say, though, not every one of them was like that. There were some really good ones, but their overall mission was to control us. The government even realized this. When they signed treaties with us, they brought in the Catholic Church to influence the way our people thought. I know we would not have signed Treaty 11 if it had not been for the Bishop who was present. My Granny asked them, "Why did they bring the Bishop?" and they answered, "Because the Bishop can't lie or steal because he works for God. He has to be telling the truth to work for God." My Granny Elizabeth told me, "So we thought they were telling truth."

But now, years later, we see it was not that way. They are every part of the grabbing of the minerals and looking for gold. We see it in North America and we see it in South America where they enslave people. In California, the Catholic priests used Native People as slaves. They are a crooked outfit and should be ashamed to show their faces around us.

When I say that not every one of them was bad, I have to mention Father Labatt in Tulita. He came from France, and Father Pochat, in Fort Rae, who came from Switzerland. They were just simple guys who came to Dene lands thinking that they would teach Natives about God. What they told me was, "The Dene People already know about God. They are closer to God than we will ever be. They are communicating with God."

The thing that surprised the Native People was that there was a Son of God, Jesus. Our People wanted to know more, because Jesus was a very good man, almost like a Dene. He didn't worry that he didn't have a bank card or a fancy Chevy truck to drive around in — he could have used one in those days in his mission. But whatever he had, he acted like a Dene. He gave food away to the people and when he would look for a place to sleep, people would say, "I have a spare place to sleep, you can sleep on my floor." Jesus wasn't like the bishops or the Pope of Rome flying around in a fancy jet or travelling in a bullet-proof car. Jesus worked with the people and that's what our People needed. Like Jesus, Father Labat and Father Pochat were simple, honest, and

Photograph of Elder Granny Tadzi looking over the Mackenzie River Valley. She had a deep knowledge and was the keeper of our memories in the stories she told us.

fun men who fit in and didn't put on any airs. If they could do something to help, they would be there. They were our People; we took them as our own.

An Elder who was very influential in my life was Granny Tadzi. She is among the group of Elders in the book. To explain, my Granny Harriet's husband was Chief Albert Wright, who was the only son of Granny Tadzi and her husband. My mom, Laura, and her always got along really well and became close friends. My mom would tell me stories about how Granny Tadzi would take her out on the traplines and how independent Granny Tadzi was. She had her own dog team and trapline, would set her own traps and nets even better than a man. She became famous that way.

She'd always talk to my mother about the old days at the time of the last ice age and the giant animals. She was a steward of the land, the keeper of all the stories of our People and of our land. Granny would point out landmarks here and there and say, "A long time ago there was a war here," or "something happened over there." Later in her life Granny Tadzi went blind and my mother would always make her supper. Mom would say to me, "Raymond, can you bring this food to Granny Tadzi with a knife and fork?" and then Granny Tadzi would talk to us about the last ice age and the dangerous animals like the saber-toothed tigers and the North American lions. We were shocked to learn that lions would use the Dene People as food.

These stories came through the ages from Elders to young ones from the first Dene People who experienced them. That's our history books because we didn't have written language. Written language would not have worked for us because we could not travel around carrying libraries. Oral tradition keeps important things in your mind, so you are carrying thousands of years of memory. You should be able to repeat word by word what they said. That's how the knowledge is carried forward.

Another thing Elders talk about in their stories is crossing a big body of salt water, so that possibly means the Bering Sea. We know that between Siberians and us, we have DNA and language similarities on both sides. We are both the same connection of People. The deep knowledge and memory from Granny Tadzi and other Elders goes back tens of thousands of years.

GOING BACK now to the film *We Remember,* Sarah Stewart, editor of this book, transcribed all the words of the Elders as collected for the film, as well as collected the words of Mary Wilson, who was not in the film. Extra footage shot for the film has been lost, but Sarah's transcriptions of the Elders' words — and Bella Ross and Sarah Jerome's translation into Gwich'in Dene language — remain a precious chronicle of their times. Many of the interviews you see and hear in the film are covered in more detail in this book.

I wish to thank my film crew who were great to work with and taught me to listen, and then to listen some more, think and then speak. *We Remember* went on to win Best Documentary Feature at the 1980 American Indian Film Awards in San Francisco, California. A thousand people gave us a standing ovation at the Palace of Fine Arts, that's when I knew we had won. It has been pointed out to me that I was the first Dene film director and so this film is the first award-winning film by a Dene director. We made a little history and had some fun along the way. As every film director knows, we cannot do it by ourselves, many thanks to my People, Elders, and the CBC film crew. Mahsi.

Mahsi Sarah Stewart, who edited the book and Mahsi Lorene Shyba, who remastered the film and also published this book. Colette Poitras has written a very moving afterword in the book that shows how, as Indigenous Peoples, we can learn the truth and build understanding through the stories told by our Elders. Mahsi Colette Poitras.

I wish to leave my last words for the native youth for the future across our country. When we began making the *We Remember* film that also became the text for his book, I was blessed to work with Elders from the Sahtú and Gwich'in regions, some of them my relatives, family and others who took me under their wing and graciously shared with me their stories for you to hear. They spoke with truth, integrity and humour about a time we will never see again. They encouraged me always with patience and I will never forget that. They are all gone now but I want their words to live forever, to teach you and future generations of Canadians, both Indigenous and non-Indigenous across the country about Dene history, culture and perspective.

Our People are the 'true children of nature' who sought and understood the mysteries that I spoke briefly about. There's more, but you need to find it for yourself as it will guide you — the power is all there in nature, it never left. Find it for yourself with your Elders and use it to do good, always.

It is always important to remember that our People need our voices to be heard in our own lands, in Canada and across the world. This award, I dedicate to the Elders and to Native youth, who are very important to the future of our country.

In my final words, I bow my head to thank Newet'sine — The One Who Made the World, the Creator of us all for everything in my life. Mahsi,

— Raymond Yakeleya, 2020.

The Dene Nation

Sarah Stewart

We Remember was a ground-breaking and award-winning documentary film based on the memories of Elders in the Mackenzie Valley. It was made by Raymond Yakeleya, a talented and professional filmmaker, who was just 24 years old when he travelled the Mackenzie Valley, talking to Elders and recording their memories for his film. My husband, filmmaker Bill Stewart, and I had just moved to Yellowknife, NWT in 1978. It was a dream come true to be living in a community where we got to know Indigenous people who were still speaking their own language, many still living a traditional life. Bill was the film editor for *We Remember* and Bill and Raymond became good friends. Over the years they worked on many other productions together.

At the time they were making *We Remember,* I had three children who were four years old and under, so I was a stay-at-home mother. Even so, I wanted to learn everything I could about the North and the people and I also wanted to contribute to Raymond's project.

We Remember, the movie, was only an hour long but more than twenty-four hours of interviews had been collected. What was to happen to those stories? Raymond, Bill and I discussed preserving the Elder's words and their witness to historical events in a book. I planned to use all the hours of interviews and also to illustrate their stories with both archival and modern pictures with specially photographed portraits of the Elders. In addition, I was fortunate to meet Elder Mary Wilson. Although she was not in the film, she wanted to share some of her memories of residential school and how she grew up — an interview that made a special addition to the book.

I never knew the other Elders in person, but I came to know them through their stories that moved me in extraordinary ways.

Their words took me on a journey of understanding, filled me with the greatest respect and admiration for their strength in overcoming challenges. My horizons were broadened as I learnt about life through their wisdom, and I was uplifted by their humour. It was a privilege to be part of this project. Many people in the local community lent photographs and their support. A list is included in the acknowledgements at the end of the book.

The Elders' vision for this book was always to have it translated into the two languages of the Elders, Gwich'in and North Slavey. Funding was granted to the South Slavey Language Research Institute and the Institute coordinated the translation of the manuscript into Gwich'in. Sadly the Institute was unable to complete the project and the book languished and eventually stalled.

Despite our efforts to raise interest in publishing the book, it seemed the time was never right and no one was interested. Although a commercial publisher wanted to publish the book it was strictly on their terms which meant no Dene languages and virtually no photographs would be included.

Years went by but Bill, Raymond and I never lost faith that one day *We Remember* would be published in book form. How much more precious it is today now that the Elders have all left this world and all we have are memories.

I have remained the guardian of the photographs and the dog-eared type-written copy of the manuscript. The original manuscript was swallowed up in some government building somewhere. The computer discs are so out of date and degraded they are unreadable. It seems as though at the eleventh hour, the value of this oral history has been recognized and valued for the treasure it is. If Bill were still alive, he would be delighted, as am I, that *We Remember* is finally being published as a book, with Dene language and photographs in place.

The Dene Nation

Dene Elders tell us that, in the beginning, Earth was a ball of fire. The Dene were pure spirits hovering over its surface waiting for Earth to be in readiness for their birth. Dene People believe that they are one with the land.

The Dene are part of the Athabaskan language family of North America. The territory of this language family stretches from the Bering Sea to Arizona. Dene means "the People" in Slavey, in Gwich'in it is Dinjii. In Navajo the word is Dine, in Apache Nde.

The Dene groups who live in the Canadian North and Alaska are the Gwich'in who live in the Mackenzie and Yukon River Deltas; the Sahtú (North Slavey) living along the Mackenzie River near Great Bear Lake; Denesuline (Chipewyan) who live east of Great Slave Lake; the Tłıchǫ (Dogrib) and T'atsaot'ine (Yellowknives) who live north of Great Slave Lake; the Deh Cho (South Slavey) who live southwest of Great Slave Lake. Historically the Gwich'in were called Loucheux and Elders in the book sometimes use this term for their people.

There are eleven official languages in the Northwest Territories of which five are Dene languages; Gwich'in, North Slavey, Chipewyan, Tłıchǫ Yatıì (Dogrib), and South Slavey. The Elders who shared their stories that appear in this book were speakers of Gwich'in and North Slavey.

In 1975, the Dene declared themselves as a Nation within Canada with the right to self-determination. They uphold the rights and interests of the Dene particularly the Dene use and occupation of their land they call Denendeh.

The Dene Nation has been in at the forefront in programs concerning health, education, community development, legal issues, land and resource development, and communications. The organization continues to work towards self-government and recognition of Indigenous rights and territory in Canada and the United States.

—Sarah Stewart, 2020

The Métis Experience

Colette Poitras

THE STORIES recounted in *We Remember the Coming of the White Man* are both heartfelt and poignant. By sharing their own stories, each Dene Elder adds to a collective truth and demonstrates a history that many Canadians do not know.

As a Métis librarian, I work to record and share the stories—ones that many Canadians have not heard before. Dene Elders have shared their stories within the pages of this book and I honour them. To understand Canadian history, it is important that we listen to their stories now. It is time we listen with our ears, with our minds, and perhaps most importantly, with our hearts.

As Indigenous People, our worldview is grounded in respect, reciprocity, and relationality. All things in nature are related, we are all related. Our relationality includes a special connection to the land. To remove us from the land is to remove a large part of our identity. It is our food source and it is our grounding. We have physical, social, spiritual, and cultural ties to the land as Indigenous Peoples. Colonization aimed to sever this connection; in many cases, we lost our kinship ties and relationships. For us, these are critical to living a good life.

I have been invited to contribute to this book as a Métis woman whose family history holds many of the same truths as the Dene. Métis history in Canada pre-dates Canadian confederation by centuries. Similar to the Dene Elders' descriptions of pre-colonial times, I have heard that while life was hard, it was good. This way of life followed the seasons. Families would travel together to live on the land, and everyone had a job and a place during the hunting, harvesting, and winter seasons. Labour was intensive and required everyone to participate, no matter age or gender. There was a sense of ethics and morality embedded within community. As Métis, we had the Laws of the Buffalo Hunt

Louis Riel (centre, seated) shown here with councillors of his provisional government in Red River, Man, 1870.

Photo: Library and Archives Canada.

to govern ourselves. As with the Dene, truth telling, reciprocity, sharing and kindness were key to survival.

As I have noted, within Indigenous communities, kinship ties and relationships equate to the worldview. It is those ties, which guides behaviour and demonstrates the values held within the community. Within our communities, we ask each other "where are you from, who are your people?" From there, we know how we relate to each other. These go beyond blood relations and include those who have been adopted in and those who have become kin by an ongoing relationship. These kinship networks and ways of relating surpass all other ways. Within the pages of the book, Jim Sittichinli remarks in this type of relating, "that's the Native way" (p.111). This is very different from the way settler, Canadian society operates.

Because of the cultural norms and values within Indigenous communities, a person's word was their honour. Sarah Simon notes, "The old people taught us how to live the right kind of life.

We respected them and listened carefully when the old stories were told." Jim Sittichinli confirms this: "The Elders taught the young people not to tell lies. They knew it was wrong" (p.127). This is an important denotation, as the people at the time did not anticipate unfulfilled promises. The colonial settler government was interested in "progress," which meant access to farmland and natural resources for use by a new settler population. Because of this, the Treaties were not negotiated in good faith by the Crown.

As with Métis history, the Dene Elders remember that despite a verbal promise, the Crown did not feel obliged to fulfill any promises made that were not written down. In the chapter "Treaty 11," the Elders note that there were promises made that no one could take the land, as well as promises for perpetual right to hunt and fish. Ultimately, false promises such as these ultimately led to the both the Métis and the Dene's dispossession from their land.

Indian residential, industrial, and convent schools severed the kinship ties and relations for Indigenous Peoples (the way we relate to each other). The Dene Elders note that they were unable to speak in their language. This was part of a larger plan for cultural genocide. Mary Wilson remembers that "Everything was so strange; the people, the language, the place" (p.147). When she was finally allowed to go home, Mary could not remember what her mother looked like and was unable to communicate with her parents. In addition to this, the unfulfilled promises by the colonial government of Canada led to a myriad of health issues new to us as Indigenous Peoples, which have been caused by starvation, disease, resource extraction, and addictions. In the chapter entitled "The Sickness," the Dene Elders within the pages of this book explain this history very eloquently.

My own Métis ancestors first conflicted with the Crown in the early 1800s over Indigenous rights during the Pemmican War, which precipitated the Victory of the Frog Plain (also known as the Battle of Seven Oaks). Many have stated that this was the beginning of the new Michif, otherwise known as the Métis Nation. As Métis people, we have a distinct language (Michif), governance structure, flag, music, dance, food, and clothing. My family's struggles continued during the Red River Resistance in 1869–1870 after which time new settlers from eastern Canada displaced Métis at the Red River (in current day Manitoba). My family moved westward towards their relations. While my direct ancestors moved to the Edmonton and Camrose area, at the same time in 1885 at Batoche (present day Saskatchewan), Métis land and way of life was threatened again, and we organized the Northwest Resistance. The Métis simply wanted to be able to maintain their homes and way of life.

Up against hundreds of soldiers and armed militia, the Métis were defeated and again dispossessed of their lands. Called rebels and traitors by the Crown, and not allowed the same rights as the "new Canadians," my ancestors continued to move westward again. Instead of Treaty negotiations with Métis people as a collective, the federal government devised the "Scrip" system, which was negotiated with individuals; Scrip was contrary to the traditional ways of the Métis. Many have noted that this was a land/money grant system laden with fraud. Scrip served to further dispossess Métis peoples of the lands they occupied and with it, our Indigenous rights. A new land base for Métis opened up in St. Paul (in what is now Alberta). Eventually, the Catholic Oblate missionaries had deemed that this was a failure and that the land should be opened up for white settlers. My family was again dispossessed of land and relationships. Because of this history, my father grew up in the hills outside of Elk Point, Alberta.

Despite years of marginalization and discrimination, Métis are a strong and resilient people. Kinship ties were and are still very strong within our community. In spite of Canadian nation building and settler colonialism, which repeatedly dispossessed us of our land and thereby our ways of being and knowing and our relationships, we continued to resist and remain political. The Métis continue to be strongly interrelated to the land and each other as Indigenous Peoples.

This is the Dene Elders' story. This is my story. It is my father's and his ancestor's story. This is our story.

In order to heal and move forward, we need to acknowledge

the truth about what happened in the past. We need to listen to these stories. The Dene Elders note that we need to look for the future. They also note that before doing so, we need to first remember and cherish our past. In the chapter "Time of Change," the Elders note that the children need to be educated, however to be whole, we need to teach our children about the land, the language, and about their culture. Together, we need to regain the relationships that have been severed through colonial impacts. As Indigenous Peoples, we need access to our traditional land to restore our ways of knowing and being together. Children need to start living their lives the way their ancestors lived and regain a physical, social, spiritual, and cultural connection to the land.

These connections are intertwined in healing and in living our best life. Being our true selves, being proud of our culture, reconnecting with our ways, knowing, and being are key to living the good life. Mary Wilson states that the "happiest time in my life was when I finally found the way back to the life I had before" (p. 246). John Blondin notes that his "grandfather taught me and I really thank him for that. I made a good life for myself. I hope the young generation will have the same" (p. 249). Connecting to the land connects Indigenous Peoples to our culture, our relations, and our worldview.

Dene culture and Métis culture are beautiful and related in this way. As Indigenous peoples, we are all related. There is room in our circle for all of our nations.

All Canadians are enriched by the stories in this collection. Up to this point, Canadians have been deprived of this Indigenous knowledge and history. By listening to these stories, we take a step together towards reconciliation. We are learning the truth and building an understanding. We are nurturing respect and reciprocity. We are honouring our relations in a good way.

Thank you, *Hiy Hiy, Marsee, Mahsi Cho,* All my relations.

—Colette Poitras, 2020

Ox cart train at Fort Smith, 1870.

Photo: Minnesota Historical Society Collection

Red River carts.

Photo: Minnesota Historical Society Collection

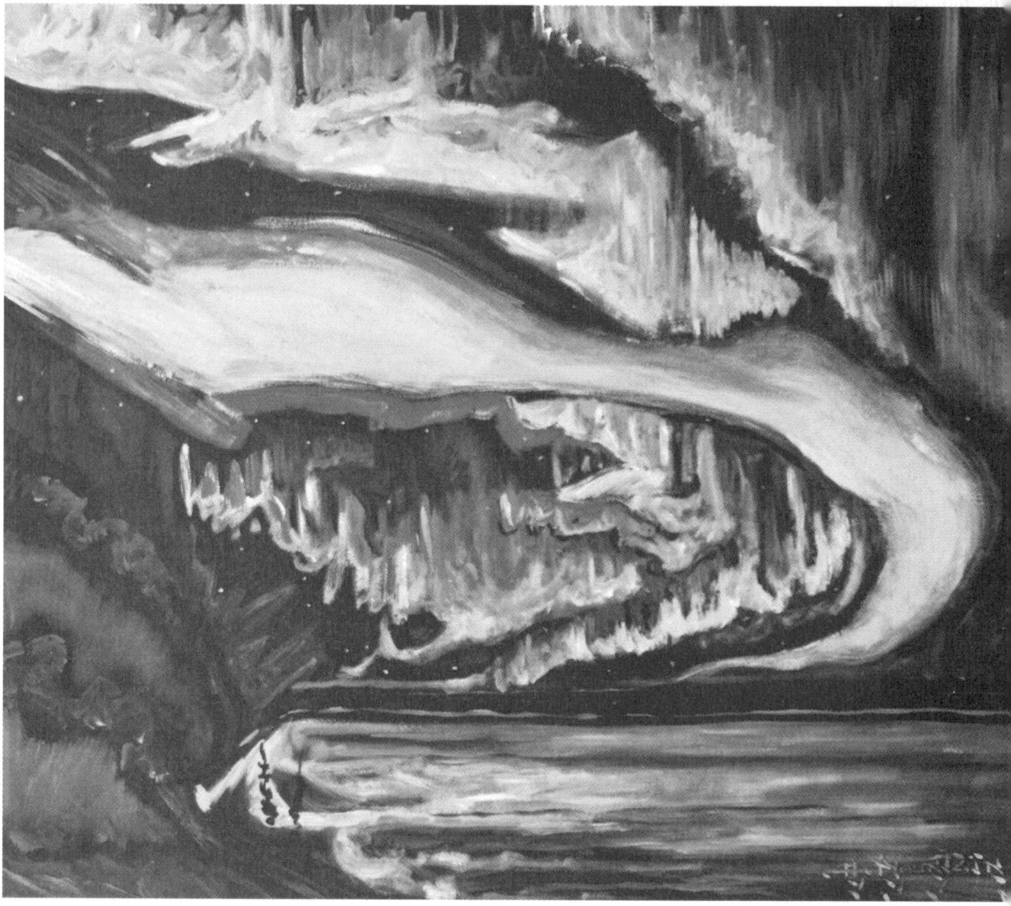

The Power and the Glory! Antoine Mountain.

These Rayuka, northern lights, seen all
over the North, are also understood to be the spirits of the dead —
those who have passed onto the Spirit World before their time,
by accident or other way.
They are neither here on Mother Earth nor in
the Great Beyond, like restless energy.
—Antoine

Part II

The Elders Remember

Elizabeth Yakeleya

Sarah Simon

Mary Wilson

Joe Blondin

John Blondin

Isadore Yukon

Johnny Kaye

Jim Edwards Sittichinli

Peter Thompson

Andrew Kunnizzi

Andrew Kunnizzi with his wife and grandson.
Photo: Dept of Information GNWT.

The Elders

ALL ARE NOW DECEASED

Elizabeth Yakeleya

Elizabeth Yakeleya (née Blondin) a Willow Lake Dene, was born in 1906 in Norman Wells *(Tlegohli)* and was educated at the convent in Fort Providence *(Zhahti Koe)*. In 1925 she married Johnny Yakeleya and they had twelve children.

Sarah Simon

Sarah Simon (née Stewart), Gwich'in, was born in the Delta on the Mackenzie River *(Deh Cho)* in 1901. She married James Simon, who was later ordained an Anglican minister. Sarah travelled with James to Yukon as a missionary and served her people for many years as a mid-wife, nurse and interpreter. She translated for government officials, doctors and for her Chief, Johnny Kaye. In June 1982 she received the Commissioner's Award for her service to her people and community. Sarah Simon died in 2001. She was 100 years old.

Mary Wilson

Mary Wilson, Slavey, was born in 1920 in Fort Good Hope *(K'asho Got'ine)* and was educated in the convent school in Aklavik. She lived in Yellowknife and worked for the Dene Nation.

Photos of Sarah Simon and Mary Wilson, Native Press, Yellowknife.

Joe Blondin

John Blondin

Isadore Yukon

Johnny Kaye

Joe Blondin, Slavey, was born in 1914 in Norman Wells. He was a trapper and hunter and was for many years a pilot with Northern Transportation Company. He was well known as a fiddle player and raconteur. He lived in Norman Wells *(Tlegohli).*

John Blondin, Willow Lake Dene, was born in 1903 in Norman Wells and lived in Fort Norman *(Tulita).* He was a hunter and trapper for all of his life. John Blondin is Elizabeth Yakeleya's brother.

Isadore Yukon, Slavey, was born in 1920 and was raised close to Fort Norman *(Tulita).* He and other Dene Leaders founded the settlement of Fort Franklin *(Deline)* where he was the mayor. He was a trapper and hunter and also a pilot with the Northern Transportation Company. In 1974, he was awarded the Order of Canada.

Johnny Kaye (Kyikavichik), Gwich'in, was born at Old Crow Flats *(Teechik)* in 1891 and died in Fort McPherson *(Teet'lit Zheh)* in January 1982. He was the Headman in Fort McPherson and was one of the two men who signed Treaty 11 in 1921 on behalf of the Gwich'in People. He was the Chief of Fort McPherson from 1948 to 1960. He was also a hunter, a trapper, a special constable with the RCMP for three years and a church warden. His portrait hangs in the community hall in Fort McPherson which is named in his memory.

Photo of Isadore Yukon, Native Press, Yellowknife.

Jim Edwards Sittichinli

Peter Thompson

Andrew Kunnizzi

Jim Edwards Sittichinli, Gwich'in, was born in 1908 and lived in Aklavik. He was one of nine children born to Edward and Annie Shadah Sittichinli. He grew up on the land around Fort McPherson *(Teet'lit Zheh)* hunting, fishing and trapping. In 1933, he married Julia Greenland. They moved to Aklavik, where they stayed for many years and raised a large family. After the death of his father, Edward Sittichinli, Jim began his training for the ministry. He was ordained in 1943 and served for 30 years. In 1960, he was ordained a priest in the Anglican Church and assumed charge of the mission and All Saints Cathedral in Aklavik.

Peter Thompson, Gwich'in, was born in 1983 and died October 1979. ¬He lived in Fort McPherson *(Teet'lit Zheh)* where he was a hunter and trapper.

Andrew Kunnizzi was born in 1892. He was a hunter and trapper, living in the Dawson region of the upper Peel Watershed. Many of his stories about the Yukon are preserved in the COPE Collection at the Northwest Territories Archives, which are located at the Prince of Wales Northern Heritage Centre in Yellowknife. He was a member of the party that retraced the Dawson Patrol route from Fort McPherson *(Teet'lit Zheh)* to Dawson, Yukon, in February 1970. He also worked for the Anglican Church for many years and was a full-time catechist.

Photos of Jim Edwards Sittichinli,
Peter Thompson and Andrew Kunnizzi,
Native Press, Yellowknife.

Gwich'in Dene spelling system,
devised by Richard Mueller in the 1960s.

Vowels

a	e	i	o	u
[a]	[e]	[i]	[o]	[u]
aa	ee	ii	oo	uu
[aː]	[eː]	[iː]	[oː]	[uː]

Consonants

b	ch	ch'	d	dr	dh	ddh	dj	dl
[p]	[tʃʰ]	[ʧ']	[t]	[ʈ]	[ð]	[tθ]	[tʃ]	[tɬ]
dz	f	g	gw	gh	ghw	h	k	kw
[ts]	[f]	[k]	[kʷ]	[ɣ]	[ɣʷ]	[h]	[kʰ]	[kʷʰ]
kh	khw	k'	l	ł	m	n	nd	nh
[x]	[xʷ]	[k']	[l]	[ɬ]	[m]	[n]	[^{n}d]	[n̥]
nj	r	rh	s	sh	shr	t	t'	th
[^{n}dʒ]	[ɹ]	[ɹ̥]	[s]	[ʃ]	[ʂ]	[tʰ]	[t']	[θ]
tth	tth'	tl	tl'	tr	tr'	ts	ts'	v
[tθʰ]	[tθ']	[tɬʰ]	[tɬ']	[ʈʰ]	[ʈ']	[tsʰ]	[ts']	[v]
w	y	z	zh	zhr	'			
[w]	[j]	[z]	[ʒ]	[ʐ]	[ʔ]			

Notes: In the book, English language adapts for
the Indigenous text, but is not always in the same story order.

When the text was first produced in 1978, the Gwich'in Dene People were most commonly known as the Loucheux. When Elders spoke to Raymond Yakeleya in 1978, they referred to their People as Loucheux.

---

1. *Early Days*

Yeʔeenoo daiʔ. "Tthak dinjii nihzhit gwidindaii". Jii Jim Sittichinli ako dinuh.

"They lived by sharing with one another."

— Jim Sittichinli

Photo: Raymond Yakeleya

Nan Kak. Jii nakhwonant kat gwiintl'oh gat'iinihdhan. Aii t'at nakhwo zhii, sizhuu. Nakhwonant kat gwiintl'oh gat'iiniidadhan. Jii nan t'at gwik'iighe? gwiidindaii.

Aii ts'at zheh gwidhoh niidiichin dai?, ah chan nakhwo datchanchyah niiih. Aat'oo ts'at aih aatsii, ts'at gyah aatsii.

Shinant kat dak t'ihch'uh. Shreendit srii dak needaa?ah. Jidii gwinzhih tthak kak srii nii?aih.

Dzhii chan ts'at dats'an nał?in. Jii geenjit nakhwonant duk needaa?ah.

Shii kheenjit gwizraih t'ijihnuh kwah. Nakhwo k'eejit kat eenjit chan t'igwinuh. Dinjii tthak eenjit chan. Aachin łoo nihts'at iidaalih kwah. Tthak nichaa, nihjuu iidaalih. Jii Elizabeth Yakeleya dinuh.

Nan Kak (The Land)

I sure love my land my son,
That's our food.
We love our land,
That's our heart.

And when we put the tent up,
We take branches and that's our floor.
Birch we use for snowshoes,
Or snares for rabbits.
I am proud of my land.

In the springtime, when the sun rises,
It shines on the green leaves and flowers,
Willows, grass and slough.
I see the ducks and the birds.
That's the way I am proud of my land.

I don't say this only for me.
It's for all our young ones in the North,
Or where our people are.
We are not strangers to one another.
We are all brothers and sisters.

— Elizabeth Yakeleya

Jii gwiiniik'oo nant kak dant vadzaih kan tr'igwindaii, aii gwit'atr'idahnch'uh. Ye?eenoo dai?, ahthaii chan ts'at nin hah gwiiyee?an goonlih kwah, ezhit dai?, dinjii zhigwiłts'ik, ts'at dinjii lat chan danaagaih... ezhit dai?, gwinniintri?. Gwid nijin ddhah tat vadzaih goonlih dai?, aii gwinoo gwiinzii gwihndaii ganałdaih. Jii t'at Jim Sittichinli zhuu danuh.

Zhik nahgehdinjik, vadzaih, dinjik hah gadhahkhaii ihłak gwigwaanah?ii kwaa ji? googaa geenjah. Nijin dinjii dinjik dhałkhaii dai?, dinjii tthak tahahshit. Adhoh chan dinjii ihłee chan tr'atsii, aii ts'at igin? chan gwint'aatr'ahchak. Chan gehndoo dinjii iizhii dinjik tthak ts'at gwintl'ahahchak. Khaii, aii chan gwik'it'ugoonch'uu. Łoo ihłak hee łoo dizhikgwiłts'ik kwah. Jii t'at Andrew Kunnizzii zhuu danuh.

Dinjii kat ee gwintl'oh gwiinzii nagaazrii guulat kat shih leii gadhahkhaii, tthak łoo giik'anahtih kwah. Dinjii tthak nihaaazrii, adhoh hah tthak giit'ajahch'uh. Jii t'at Jim Sittichinli zhuu danuh.

Ediniichii gwiyeendoo ts'at dinjii eenjit chił?ee nilii. K'ii tshi? chan ts'at iisrii vah tr'igwidjaak'ii eenjit, aii eenjit giit'ahjahch'uu. Han gwinjik neekat gwa?an dant gwizrih

Great Slave Lake Mooseskin Boat.
Photo: Glenbow Museum, Calgary, Alberta.

WE DEPEND on caribou in the North land. When animals were scarce, the people sometimes starved. That was hard times. But when there were caribou on the mountains, that was easy living and the best time in my life.

They travelled all the time and killed moose or caribou. If they killed nothing they still kept going. When a man killed a moose, he divided it up and gave it away. No money. He gave a hind quarter to this one, front quarter to that one so everybody had meat. Next time another guy will shoot the moose and he will do the same. Nobody goes hungry.

— Andrew Kunnizzi

WHEN a group of the People went to the hunting grounds some were lucky, or I should say they were good hunters. They would get more than the others but they didn't keep everything for themselves. They shared with the people who had less. They shared everything even the hides to make clothing.

— Jim Sittichinli

vitr'ahgwahʔaih. Shin gwindoo gweedhan gwizrih vuutr'agintih, gwits'at niizhit eenjit. Jidii giikhan gweheendaii zrih hah nahgahdaadal. Dinjik dreetth'an ts'at k'ii tshiʔ gahtsii. Ejiʔ niizii, aii chan k'ii tshiʔ gahtsii. Ihłak juutin ts'at neekat juutin, akoo k'ii tshiʔ dahłeii gahtsii. Diik'eetshiʔ agwahntshii niint'aii. Dinjii nidhiizrii dant, k'ii aii gwits'at naandak ts'at k'ii deechii zrih gwizhit diinch'uu. K'ii tshiʔ iizhii naandachan k'ii tshiʔ t'aanaanlik. Nehkaii ahtsii daiʔ iisrii hah naiiyahkhaii.

Aadzaii choo dhoh, aii zrih chan gyah gaatsii. Ezhit gwinoo łoo gweendoo chivyaa k'it'iinch'uu kwah. K'aii gitl'uu aii chuu zhit tshigiiyaaʔak. Nijin łuk eenjit chuu gwiinzii dant ezhit dant tshiigiiyaaʔak, łuk vizhit jaa. Łuk eenjit k'oo tr'agwahtsii. Aii gwich'ii chan k'aii gwinangwidaadhaih, łuk haan neeheedaa kwaa eenjit. K'aii ee ghoo gahtsii giiyitl'uh, vizhit gweedii chuu zhit vizhit łuk jah. Juuts'ants'at nagaazrii ts'at luk kageediʔih. Jii Jim Sittichinli zhuu danuh.

Nagwidadhat ihłak gwizhit nahgehdinjik. Khehłak t'igiinch'uh jiʔ, duuyeh shih agugwahʔaih. Jii t'at Johnny Kaye zhuu danuh.

K'ii tr'ih dinjii kat digiʔih, aii zhit nagahdahkak. Tr'iinjoo,

FLINT was very precious to the People. They used it for arrowheads, spearheads, and for lighting fires. There were only two places on the Peel River where you could get it so in the summer a few people were chosen to go there and get it because it was a long way inland. They packed out as much as they could carry and that was a year's supply. They also made arrowheads out of moose legs, or from a horn if they had a good one.

A person would have ten arrows with about twenty or thirty arrowheads. These worked like bullets. The hunter followed the caribou and when he shot it, the arrowhead stayed in but the shaft flew out. He would pick it up and use another arrowhead which he would have in his bag. When the animal was wounded he used his spear.

They also used snares for big animals which they made out of bull moose skin which is a good strong hide. In those days there were no fish nets like today. They used to make traps out of willow which they knitted together to make a fence. Then where the water was right, they drove in sticks and wove the willow between them. They left a gap and enclosed it with fencing to make the trap. At the entrance they stuck pointed willows so the fish could not get out once they were caught. They also used to make a big round loop and wove willow into a basket. They put it where the fish would come and catch them. So that's the way they used to live, hunting and fishing.

— *Jim Sittichinli*

THEY travelled all year long. If they stayed in one place it would be too hard to get food.

— *Johnny Kaye*

Tinite, Sahtú (Slavey) shaman making snowshoes.
Photo: National Museums of Canada.

Han jiʔ khaii hee nahtr'ahdinjik ts'at vadzaih kan tr'igwindaii, niiii gaii tr'ahtsii, ts'at adhoh chan tr'ahtsii. Dazhoo hah chan tr'ahdaajaa chan gahtsii. Shih hee chan adhoh hah nahgiihaadaazhaa gahtsii. Aklavik ts'at Teetl'it Zheh gwik'ideetak ddhah tat nahgadaadal dant vadzaih gadhakhaii. Gweendoo vadzaih kheʔ goonlii kwaa ezhit gwindoo nahtr'aadaazhaa giits'at ahtsii, niivyaa chan gahtsii. K'eejit kat, aii geenjit gwitr'it t'agwaaʔii, anjoo kat chan geenjit łuk gat'agwahʔii. Jii Jim Sittchinli zhuu danuh.

Ganałdaii, shiyoʔghwon kat tr'oochit zheh gwidhoh gooviinkat. Aii gwitshih daiʔ, adhoh niivyah gidiʔii, ts'at vadaachan goonlih, giiyah nahgiihaadaazhik. Ezhit daiʔ gwinoo niivyaa ihłak nitshii tr'ahtsii, zheh k'oo neekant geenjit, uundoo gwitl'at chan

THEY had birchbark canoes which the men paddled. The women and children walked along the shore. They would follow behind for two hundred miles, all the way up to the Snake River.

— *Andrew Kunnizzi*

THERE were no skidoos, we had to use dogs. There were no kickers. When we went in the bush we had to paddle... paddle all the time. We made little boats out of moose skins, just for one family.

— *Jim Sittichinli*

IN THE wintertime the people hunted caribou all along the Peel River and made drymeat and worked with the skins. They made fur clothing of caribou.

In the summertime they got the skins for clothing. They used to travel in the mountains between Aklavik and Fort McPherson where the caribou calved.

Before the new caribou hair has grown in and when the old hair has just come out the skin is bare. Then it is good for clothing and for tents too.

The young people did that while the old people fished in the fishing places.

— *Jim Sittichinli*

I CAN remember my parents first bought a tent. Before that they had a caribou skin tent and poles to put it up. They carried the poles and cover tied together in a bundle everywhere. We used to make one big tipi for two families with a fire in the middle. Everyone worked together.

— *Andrew Kunnizzi*

Camp at Fort Simpson (Liidli Kue), 1930.
Photo: Public Archives Canada.

Travelling with dogs and canoes.
Photo: National Photography Collection Public Archives Canada.

Tipis made of caribou hide at Great Slave Lake .
Photo: Provincial Archives of Alberta E Brown Collection.

Fort McPherson (Teet'lit Zheh) in the early days.
Photo: National Photography Collection Public Archives Canada.

gwijuuk'an?. Jii Andrew Kunnizzii zhuu danuh.

Vadzaih dhoh niivyaa nilii ee vidaachan goonlii iidi?in?. Shik nahjaazhik niivyaa niidaachii eenjit. Jii Johnny Kaye zhuu danuh.

Tr'oochit Hudson Bay tyah chan ts'at vizhit goonli? hah k'agilik, aii gwik'iighe? vizhit vaka?tr'ahch'uu goodlit. Aii gwitshih gwinoo kwan? ts'at vakatr'ahch'uu gwizrih. Shin hee etrik gwijuuk'an?, chii gwizhit tr'ilik, aii zhit tr'ahch'uh, vizhit shih tr'ilii. Chuu vizhit tr'injaa, gwik'iighe? khant vir. Jii t'at Andrew Kunnizzii ako danuh.

One of the Last Tipis, 1927.
Photo: National Photography Collection Public Archives Canada.

We had a caribou skin tipi and it had a frame. We carried the frames with us all the time and used them when we set up camp.

— Johnny Kaye

Hudson Bay brought in pans and copper kettles but before that we had nothing to boil meat in so it was just roast ... roast ... roast. In summertime we used to put a skin or a moose's stomach into a hole and put water in it, then hot hot rocks. We kept the rocks clean and were careful not to burn the skin. That was how we boiled meat.

— Andrew Kunnizzi

EDITOR'S SIDEBAR: ABOUT "FURS AND GUNS" CHAPTER

IN 1798 ALEXANDER MACKENZIE, in search of the North West Passage, was the first outsider to paddle down the Mackenzie River to the Arctic Ocean. As a Bourgeois of the North West Company, he began to trade for fur with the people he encountered. The first trading post was built in 1796 at Fort Resolution and over the years there were many more in the Mackenzie Valley. The sites of the trading posts were places where the Dene met each year in the summer.

The Hudson's Bay Company followed the North West Company. After many years of bitter trading rivalry, the Hudson's Bay Company amalgamated with the North West Company in 1821. Now they held a trading monopoly that lasted for the next hundred years.

Andrew Kunnizzi's account tells of the first contact with white people close to what is now Fort McPherson. This event must have occurred prior to 1840, when the trading post at Fort McPherson was founded. The second account, by Joe Blondin, tells of a meeting with fur traders at Sucker Creek, close to what is now Fort Norman. The encounter would have occurred before 1805.

Many of the early traders were French and Scots who made the new land their home, marrying Native women and raising large families. Trade goods, such as guns, knives, axes, and kettles were luxuries that quickly became necessities. The people traded meat, fish or fur for these. Debt became a way of life when fall supplies had to be paid for with fur trapped the following spring.

After the First World War trapping became a lucrative business and there was a massive influx of white trappers. In 1927 alone, three million dollars' worth of fur came from the North. When the Government introduced regulations in 1938, it was too late. Dene hunting and trapping grounds were depleted, fur prices had fallen, fur traders and white trappers had returned home rich or else turned to mining and prospecting. It was many years before there was a recovery but today trapping is a major source of income for the Dene. – *Sarah Stewart*

2. *Fur, Guns, First Contact*

Aii guuzhik zrit Hudson Bay tthak nahgwidintl'oh, jidii gwits'an giftsaii eenjit. Aii tl'ee gwindoo tr'igooheekat eenjit. Jii t'at Andrew Kunnizzi ako dinuh.

"And all the time Hudson Bay wrote down what they were giving away and they made them pay later on. I noticed that. They didn't give anything away."

— *Andrew Kunnizzi*

Tl'yah k'it t'iinch'uu, aii chan jidii tsal nilih ts'at nan kak nigiiniinlih, juu doh?ii nakhwagahnuh. Jii dahaa?ah, guuvaadinuh, ts'eet'at tshi? zhit jaadhohk'an? nakhwagahnuh. Aii gwik'iighe? itjidhiłk'an? gahshindaih.

Ezhit dai? gwinoo, adhoh thał ik hah tr'idi?ii, vicheet'it kwah, diicheet'it tr'iheelaa łoo tr'idi?ih kwah. Aii ts'eet'at dhoh kat gitr'iłtl'ih. Aii ts'at gee?ał, guuzhik nihk'eehaadaadhak. Edhitl'ii dititih ditsik giik'anit'ii, tr'iinjoo ts'at giiyahtsii, thoh giiyaa?ah eenjit.

Aii guuzhik zrit Hudson Bay tthak nahgwidintl'oh, jidii gwits'an giłtsaii eenjit. Aii tl'ee gwindoo tr'igooheekat eenjit. Jii t'at Andrew Kunnizzi ako dinuh.

Tr'oochit oonjit tr'anah?ii, Fort Simpson di? ts'at dant, shizheh goo?aii. Aii dats'at teechik dant. Tr'ihchoo zhit k'adadał, guutr'anaajat ts'at gwitat gwits'at tr'ichuujil. Dinjii, aii zrih naajat kwah, aii zrih ezhit naa?eh.

Dinjii ihłee guuveenjit łehteedi?deeliaa, aii ts'at gwinoo natoghwotjaa guuvahnuu. Aii dinjii ihłee diik'ee vits'an tr'ałtsaii, naajat kwaa eenjit. Aii ts'at nits'oo nin eenjit khyah tr'oodlii, aii gahviidandai? giiniidhan, aii ts'at nits'oo ts'at

THE Loucheux had never seen anyone else before, not a Slavey or a white man. They were at a fish trap catching fish going up stream when they saw one or maybe two York boats coming right up to their fish camp. They thought that bad men were going to kill them, so the women and children ran into the bush and whoever was brave enough stood on the shore and waited for them to land.

"Oh by gosh! They're all white with brown hair! Never seen anyone like them before." They were sure scared. These white people made a sign to show that they were friendly so everyone quietened down.

They had a Slavey interpreter so they could talk to us and they asked to see the Chief. They had something with them like a coil of rope which they put on the shore and cut up into little pieces and gave to each man.

"What are we going to do with this?"

"You need a clay pipe. You put it in there and smoke it."

And that's how I learnt to smoke my pipe.

Well in those days the people had caribou or moose skin pants but no pockets. They didn't have anything to put in their pockets anyway. So they tied a little bit of tobacco to their belt and it just swung around as they walked. They cut up little strips of red stroud for the women. That was for a belt.

And all the time Hudson Bay wrote down what they were giving away and they made them pay later on. I noticed that. They didn't give anything away.

— *Andrew Kunnizzi*

THE FIRST WHITE MEN were seen down from Fort Simpson, near where my cabin is now at Sucker Creek. They came down in a scow.

When the people saw them coming, they all headed into the bush. Only one old fellow was brave enough to stay at the camp when they landed. They had an interpreter with them and he hollered for them to come back. One by one they did.

datchan khyah tr'ahtsii, akoo daguugahnuu. Iitsii khyah ezhit gwinoo kwah. Aii ts'at tyah chan gootl'agiiʔaih ts'at diik'ee tshiʔ chan muzzleloader eenjit guuts'an gałtsaii, ts'at diik'ee kwanʔ. Ezhit nugwidadhat gwinoo, nin dhoh dahłeii gahtsaii, aii diginliʔ hah gehdichii, aii ihłogwinliʔ juutin gwits'at gwizrih gahgidandaii. Aii nin dhoh nik'oo gitilii, ihłogwijuutin ahłeii, gał nik'itoh t'igiiyełik. Aii gwik'iigheʔ daananch'uu giiyahdandaih. Aii tl'ee gehndoo nugwidadhat, oonjit khehkaiʔ k'anadik dant, gał danaach'uu gehjuutin gwik'iigheʔ nin dhoh danaanch'uu hah gahdandaih. Aii gwik'iigheʔ gik'anaanjik. Jii t'at Joe Blondin ako dinuu.

Hudson Bay tr'oochit muzzleloader k'agilik. Aii t'at tr'oochit diik'ee shiʔih. Diik'ee gwiiniidhan jiʔ, gwiintl'oh khyah tr'oodlii geenjit gwitr'it t'ugwahʔii. Iitsii khyah kwah, datchan khyah gwizrih. Hudson Bay diik'ee iiʔduk naagaathak, aii vehghee nin dhoh nihk'ehdak nitr'iinlih aii gwik'iigheʔ diik'ee diits'an tr'ahtsii. Gwik'iigheʔ nin dhoh leii gahtsii, gehndoo chan diik'ee ninjuu k'agilik. Dugwahtshii diik'ee dilii gahgwidandaih kwah, nin dhoh chan. Nin tseedhoh łoo hah gwidindaih kwah. 1920's gwinoo ezhii khehkaiʔ k'adadal. Ezhit Hudson Bay

The man who hadn't run away was given a gun as a mark of respect. Then they made it known that they wanted to barter for fur and showed the people how to make deadfalls to catch marten and mink. There were no such things as steel traps then.

Although they got nothing in return, they gave the people a couple of pails, copper pots, a couple of horns of black powder and about 50 rounds of bullets for the muzzleloader.

The people saved the fur that winter, but they didn't know how many skins they had. They just used to count on their fingers and didn't know how to count to more than ten. So they put the fur in lots of ten, took a stick that was flat on one side and put X's all along it. Every X counted as a ten.

When the manager came through with his goods the next year, he was presented with the stick so he knew how many skins there were. That was the start of bartering.

HBC, Here Before Christ as the old saying goes!

— *Joe Blondin*

HUDSON BAY brought in muzzleloaders. That was the first kind of gun I used. If you wanted to buy a gun you had to go out and work hard trapping, not with steel traps but mostly dead falls and snares. The Hudson Bay would stand the gun up and pile your fur alongside it until the fur reached to the top of the barrel. Then you could buy it. They were doing so good on that the next time they brought in guns they had longer barrels.

The people didn't know what the gun was worth. They didn't know the price of fur or the value of money. In the 1920s other traders started coming down the river. That's when we found out that Hudson Bay really cheated us in many many ways.

— *Jim Sittichinli*

gwiinleii gwizhit nanighwoganii?ak jukwaahee gik'anaanjik. Jii t'at Jim Sittichinli ako dinuh.

Muzzleloader 30 inch dilii ezhit gwinoo, aii chan tseedhoh nihkat taatr'oołih, dahdhee aii diik'ee vitshi? gwits'at. Aii tł'aa gwizrih diik'ee tr'ooviikat. Jii t'at Joe Blondin ako dinuh.

Muzzleloadeer vihkat niidhan ji?, diik'ee naagaathak, aii nin dhoh vehghee nitr'iinlih, ako dinjii kat dugahnuu, aii tł'ee gwizrih diik'ee ts'an gahtsii. Jii Johnny Kaye ako dinuh.

K'ii nahgwaan gwizrih ahtahk'eh ts'at muzzleloader aii niizhit ahtahk'eh. Aii ts'at aii dugwahtshii muzzleloader dilii gaa guuveenjit ihłoh t'ugoonch'uh kwah. Dinjii gaa lat muzzleloader hah nehkaii gahtsii, k'i? hah nahgiiyahkhaii. Jii t'at Andrew Kunnizzi ako dinuh.

Adai? gwinoo dinjii kat k'i? hah nugaazrii, gwiintł'oh shih tr'adhakhaii kwah. Aii shih ts'at nahgwan k'it t'iinch'uh kwah eenjit. Aii tł'ee gwinoo, Hudson Bay diik'ee k'agilik. Shiti?, muzzleloader uuviinkat, shigweheelaa gwitshih, aii tł'ee shint'eh vah niłzrih ts'at geh vah dhiłkhaii. Chan k'eejit kat nits'oo ts'at giizhit diik'ee kwan? giheelaa gahgidandaih. Dinjik, vadzaih, dats'an hah diik'ee tshi? nitshii, nitsal hah tr'oodahk'ee. Jii Peter Thompson ako dinuh.

First Nations boy with gun to shoot rabbits and small game.
Photo: National Photography Collection Public Archives Canada.

Muzzleloaders had about a thirty-inch barrel. They used to pile beaver skins flat on the ground. When they came level with the top of the barrel then you could buy the gun.

— *Joe Blondin*

IF YOU wanted to buy a muzzleloader, Hudson Bay stood the gun up and told the people to pile their skins up until they were level with the top of the gun.

— *Johnny Kaye*

THE arrowhead didn't go very far but the muzzleloader went further. So they were very glad to get it whatever the price. Some people wounded the animal with the muzzleloader then used their arrows to kill it.

— *Andrew Kunnizzi*

Tr'oochit, diik'ee kwanʔ vizhit t'ahʔii, aii hah ejahk'eh. Tl'ee chan ezhii diik'ee kwanʔ vizhit t'ahʔaii, aii chan vah ejahk'eh. Shaa hah geh eenjit naazrih, shitiʔ muzzleloader diʔii hah. Geh dhaakhaih kwaa, aii ts'at diik'ee hah tsiiʔiidiʔih ts'at vizhit diik'ee kwanʔ tsal aaʔih, iiduk chan ahdaak'eh. Chan vizhit diik'ee kwanʔ iidilik, vah ehjaak'eh, aii diik'ee jiidatth'ak. Jii t'at Andrew Kunnizzi ako dinuh.

Yeenoo daiʔ diik'ee kwanʔ zrih gwiinliʔ. Dinjik, vadzaih,shih hah tr'oodahk'eh, łat zhit nagal tr'ahaadal ts'at jidii tr'adhałkhaii kugwinaaʔih. Jii t'at Joe Blondin ako dinuh.

K'eejit ihłii gwinoo, Shuuʔii muzzleloader hah adahk'ee niłʔih. Datchanchyah kat dhiidii, veenjit gwiintsal t'igwiłʔin. Iitsii kanitii, jidii ddhak ałtsaii, aii tl'ee jidii ghoo nilii. Diik'ee tshiʔ kwanʔ kat yiniłghoh. Yiniłghoo tl'ee chan yinahghoh ts'at dizhanyuunjah. Ejiʔ shiyiinjah dahdhee danadlat gwits'at, chuutyah hah dizhanyuunjah. Dahłeii yah heedandaii eenjit. Diik'ee kwanʔ iitsii hah nihtat t'iinlik. Aii tl'ee t'at diik'ee tshiʔ leii gwits'at diʔih. Chidhiniintin ts'at yizhit ahdehk'eh. Gwiinzii ahdehk'eh. Aii tl'ee chan diik'ee tshiʔ leii nałtsaii. Aii ts'at

Woman stretching moose hide.
Photo: Dept of Information GNWT.

FIRST YOU put the powder in, then the wad, then shot, then wads again. After that put the primer and pull the trigger to go. My brother-in-law and I were hunting rabbit with my dad's muzzleloader. We didn't get any so we started playing with the gun. We used just a little bit of powder and shot straight up in the air. When the bullet came down, we caught it. Then we put less powder and we could hear the bullet move along in the barrel and drop right out the end!

— *Andrew Kunnizzi*

didiik'ee gwiinzii k'anahtii. Diik'ee tshiʔ dhok k'anahtii. "Ihłoh t'ohʔih shroʔ," shahnuh. Aii ts'at vadraii chijih kwah. Aii tł'ee dats'an leii k'analik, kheh chan. Shreendit, May nant ako didiʔin. Jii t'at Sarah Simon ako dinuh.

Diik'ee ihłak tr'idiʔih daiʔ, dinjii leii giiyah nidhizrih. Aii gwiintł'oh vatr'adahch'uh. Jii t'at Joe Blondin ako dinuh.

Hudson Bay chivyah chan ts'at vitł'aa hah k'agilik. Khaii, anjoo kat chivyah gitł'uh. Shin geenjit. Dinjii chivyah neekaii diʔih jiʔ, aii t'at vah gwidindaii nilii. Chivyah ihłak chinyaachuu, aii tł'ee khaanʔaii nahchuh. Tł'ee chan ihłak ts'at yik'eeʔahtrah. Akoh ts'ants'at chivyah k'aganahtii. Nijin chivyah łatchah naiiyitł'uh. Shik chivyah gwiinzii k'aganahtih. Jii t'at Jim Sittichinli ako dinuh.

Hudson Bay tr'oochit zhadant gwits'at ihłogwinliʔ ako dahdhee ookat zheh tr'oochit guugwałtsaii. Juk zrit "Zheh Gwijat goovaazhii." Tr'oochit, muzzleloader diik'ee tshiʔ, lidii ts'at daatlih, dinjii itjiich'ii chan gahtsii, aii tł'ee gwindoo, nindhoh hah nagiiyuukat. Jii t'at Johnny Kaye ako dinuh.

John Firth tr'oochit khehkaiʔ inliʔ. Itjiich'ii ookaat ahtsii. Lidii chan ts'at soogaii, łuh hah chuutyah ihłoggwinliʔ lidii, edhitł'ii

Fur Store January 1907 "J.M. Bickell's first batch value $4,000."
Photo: Provincial Archives of Alberta E. Brown Collection.

THERE was only black powder in those days and if you shot a moose, caribou, or a bear you had to run around the smoke to find out if you hit it or not.

— *Joe Blondin*

WHEN I was very young, I saw my uncle loading a muzzle-loader. I was sitting on the floor holding things for him. He had a long piece of lead and he hammered it on the anvil and made long skinny square pieces, cut them with a cutter, and put them into a dish. He ground it with a stone and soon the shots were round.

To make bullets he melted lead on the fire. When it was ready, he put it in something with a ring around it. He let it set then took it out.

He had gun powder in a horn. He put it into measuring cups that he had. He put the shot and powder, then wads and wads into the gun and then took it outside to see how it sounded. Good, so he made more shells.

Fort Norman (Tulita) in 1930s.
Photo: Hudson's Bay Company Winnipeg.

kat dishinjaa, aii t'at khaii tthak geenjit. Hudson Bay, tr'iinin kat gwitch'aa gidiʔih kwah. Ookat zheh gwits'at edhitl'ii hah tr'iinin gwitch'aa tr'ahtsii, thał chan ts'at ik hah guuhant guuveenjit ahtsii' Shitr'iinin kat guuveenjit thał, ik hah dhałtsaii, ts'at tshuh ik, tshuh thał hah. Shidinjii veenjit chan tshuh ik dhałtsaii. Nitr'aazrii geenjit nizii. Jii t'at Sarah Simon ako dinuh.

Dinjii kat, tseedhoh gidiʔih kwah. Nin dhoh ts'at nilii, łuk hah ookat gahtsii. Dinjii Johnny Kaye k'it t'iinch'uu, William Firth oonjit kat eenjit gwitr'it t'agwahʔii. Aii gwik'iigheʔ tseedhoh gidiʔih. Jii t'at Sarah Simon ako dinuh.

Aklavik, 1921.
Photo: National Photography Collection Public Archives Canada.

He had to keep his gun clean and in a good gun case. He kept all his shells separate and told me not to touch them so I didn't. He went out and brought back a big load of ducks and geese. That was in the month of May.

— *Sarah Simon*

HAVING a gun in your possession was something great eh? In a tribe of about forty or sixty people we had only one gun and everybody depended on that gun.

— *Joe Blondin*

HUDSON BAY brought in narrow net twine and in the winter the old people's job was making nets for the summer. If a person had two nets, he was a man and a half. He had to set only one net at a time and not for too long either. Then he took it out and washed it while he set the other. He mended it every time a mesh was broken. That's the way he made them last.

— *Jim Sittichinli*

Hudson Bay kat 1920's gwinoo, itjiich'ii ookat gahtsii. Ezhit dai? łoo tseedhoh ihłak gaa tr'anah?ih kwah. Dinehtl'eh dinjii eenjit kaganahtii, aii gwik'iighe? jidii dinjii gwiinzii uunkat di?ii, aii zrih itjiich'ii chan gahtsii. Aii dinjii ihłoh t'inuh dai?, shuu giduudhiłch'eeh. Nits'oo iindoo tr'eedaa gwik'it gwizrih goonlih. Jii t'at Joe Blondin akoo dinuh.

Yeenoo dai? Hudson Bay tr'ih choo hah teegah dadal, kaii k'it goodlii tthak. Dinjii ihłak juutin ts'at ihłogwinli? hah tr'ih choo gwitr'it t'igah?ii. Kaii k'it tthak geenjit. Jii t'at Joe Blondin

Teetl'it Zheh gwits'at tr'ih zhit geekah ts'at han nji? nugahdidah, Fort Smith gwits'at Hudson Bay eenjit gwadal kagitjah. Shin tthak geenjit nugahdidal. Khaiints'an jukwaahee tseedhoh gwit'ii ganah?ih kwah. Zheh gwadhoh chan ts'at gwich'aa ihłoo gwizrih nugiihadaazhaa, aii zrih guuts'an tr'ahtsih. Jii t'at Jim Sittichinli ako dinuh.

HUDSON BAY built a trading post five miles from Fort McPherson. Today they call it the Old Fort. At first when they started trading, we got tea, tobacco, soap, muzzle-loaders, shots, bullets, and black powder. Hudson Bay used to give goods out to each person but when they got fur later on they had to pay with that.

— *Johnny Kaye*

JOHN FIRTH was the Hudson Bay manager in Fort McPherson. You could buy dry goods in the store; tea, sugar, and flour. Mr. Firth had to ration it so it didn't run short. He used a cup and measured the loose tea by the cupful onto the cloth. Five cups of tea. That's for all winter.

Hudson Bay didn't have much in the way of children's clothing so most mothers made them out of material they got from the store. I made all my children's clothing, underclothes, dresses, pants, and parkas.

We insulated the parkas and pants with feathers. It is very light and good for hunting. I made them for my husband many times.

— *Sarah Simon*

PEOPLE had no money. They bought with fur, meat, or fish. People like Johnny Kaye who was a very good hunter and trapper and worked for white people. Or William Firth would have a little money.

— *Sarah Simon*

At the Hudson's Bay Post.
Frame from the film We Remember.

A great bounty of furs.
Frame from the film We Remember.

Harriet Gladue of Fort Norman (Tulita) prepares muskrat skins.
Photo: CBC North.

Fort McPherson (Teet'lit Zheh) in 1930s.
Photo: Hudson's Bay Company Winnipeg.

Dinjii kat lat ddhah ohts'aii gugwitch'in, guulat chan ehdii tat gugwitch'in. łuk chan kagidiʔih, ddhah ts'at chan gitinjik. Zheh k'oo gwiintshii, aii dachaaval neekaii gidiʔih, łaii ihłogwinliʔ hagidiʔih. November nant gwits'at gitinjik, May gwits'at. Tl'ee t'at han iinoo nagadadal ... Jii t'at Sarah Simon ako dinuh.

Zheh gwits'ee giheedidaa geenjit gwik'it goovah nugwidjaanaii kwaa ts'at chan dinjik eenjit nugaazrih. Ezhit gwinjiʔ, dinjik nant gwiinzii. Aii ts'at chan nizii tugwiłjik. Aii tl'ee nihk'it tugidiinlih, tl'il hah tl'angiiyahchoh. Jii t'at Jim Sittichinli ako dinuh.

Tr'iinjoo kat dinjik dhoh khagit'ii, giitii chan git'ih. Aii tl'ee nagiiyahtrah. Nihk'uu giiyuunjih, nitshii giiyahtsii. Dinjik dhoh ihłojuutin ts'at daankat, ako dinjik dhoh dinaanch'uu hah tr'ih choo gahtsii. Jii t'at Sarah Simon ako dinuh.

Tr'ih choo daang kat gałtsaii ts'at taaʔaii choo nihk'iitik. Aii ts'at dinjii tr'ihchoo nitsal zhit geekah. Nadanaajaa zhit geekaa. Nadanaajaa kwaa daiʔ chan. Chan taaʔaii agadanduk. Jii t'at Jim Sittichinli ako dinuh.

Teetl'it Zheh k'adadal, chan guunałʔih. Digizhehk'oo ihłogwinliʔ geetak chan nihk'iitik gidilii. Aii tl'ee dinjii kat aii tr'ihchoo khagidinlii. Adhoh gwits'at tr'igiinlii. Tr'iinjoo chan aii adhoh sritr'igiinlih. Jii t'at Sarah Simon ako dinuh.

HUDSON BAY operated on a trading basis until the early 1920s. You never saw such a thing as a dollar or even a dime. Hudson Bay kept a log book on all the people with recommendations. If you're a good hunter you're allowed so much. If you're a bum hunter you get nothing.

There was no competition, so they had a monopoly. If you raised an objection your name was mud. You were discredited so they had you either way, coming or going.

— *Joe Blondin*

ALL THE Hudson Bay's merchandise used to come in York boats. There were ten to fifteen men per boat and every fort had one.

— *Joe Blondin*

THE PEOPLE used to go up the river from Fort McPherson to get the Hudson Bay outfit from Fort Smith. It took them all summer to do that with no engine in the boat. All the way up the Mackenzie by oars, track and sail, a distance of about 1,200 miles. When they came back in the fall all those people got was an 8x10 tent or a suit of clothes. No cash.

— *Jim Sittichinli*

IN 1900, when my father, uncles, and Chief Julius were all young boys, they went over the mountains to Lapierre House, a Hudson Bay Trading Post. They were backpacking and dogpacking their belongings with them.

They met some miners there. One of them was called Doctor and he was the boss. When they were ready to come back the miners gave them some food.

Then a white man said to Francis, one of the Indians, "Let me buy your dog. I can't pack everything by myself."

"No!" said Francis, "You gave me grub and I have to pack that and it's heavy. I need my dog. Besides he's a good, obedient, strong dog and I don't want to part with him."

Teetl'it Zheh k'adadal, chan guunał?ih. Digizhehk'oo ihłogwinli? geetak chan nihk'iitik gidilii. Aii tl'ee dinjii kat aii tr'ihchoo khagidinlii. Adhoh gwits'at tr'igiinlii. Tr'iinjoo chan aii adhoh sritr'igiinlih. Jii t'at Sarah Simon ako dinuh.

.. Zhat dant gwits'at gitinjik, ehdii tat gwits'at, nugaazrii khyah chan giheedlih. Juk gweendoo gwik'it t'ugoonch'uh kwah. Ezhit gwinoo datchan khyah tr'ahtsii. Nijin nehtryuh dhałkhaii dai?.... 5 dollars. Jii t'at Andrew Kunnizzi ako dinuh.

Vadzaih eenjit łoo naazrih kwah, gwid khyah dhiididlii gah?iidindaih. Tsuk ts'at chidhee hah eenjit khyah iidadlii. Khyah ontshuh zhit daa?aii, khyah zhii, aii hah nachii da?ał. Tr'iinin chan nachii da?ak. Vaka?tr'ahch'uu chan gah?iidindaih, k'ehdanaakaii chan gah?iidindaih. Nilii chan khadiniidit'uh, troo chan iidachah, zheh gwadhoh chan nidiichii. Gwiintl'oo gwitr'it t'aa?ih. Dinjii łoo guuvah nutr'adidal kwah. Dhok gwitr'it t'ugwah?ii. Nakhwont'eh chan. Tr'iinjoo zrit digizheh gwizrih geenjit gwitr'it t'ugwah?in. Ts'at nakhwodinjii eenjit k'ediniidikaii?. Naagaii, łaaswaii, ch'oo hah dinjii nitr'aanahts'i?. Tr'iinjoo duuyeh dakaiitrii? naanahts'i?. Diitsuu diits'at gigiinkhih. Nakhwodinjii guuk'ogohdhat nuh. Nakhwodinjii nakhwotshid nilih. Jii t'at Sarah Simon ako dinuh.

But the white man kept on asking and in the end he showed him money.

"I'll give you this."

"I don't want that! What am I going to do with buttons?"

"When you get back to Fort McPherson give it to the Hudson Bay manager and he'll give you stuff for it. And on top of that I'm going to give you a sack of flour."

Now no man would carry around a fifty pound bag of flour in those days and if you bought maybe five or ten cups then you were a wealthy man. So when he saw this bag of flour he thought it was a really good deal. So he took it and sold his dog.

Well the Indians had heard of gold and they called it red rock. So all the way home, every time they stopped, he took the money out of his pocket and said, "Look at my gold. Just one piece is very valuable. Look how much I have."

He is so happy.

When he got back home, he went to the store and gave it to the boss. 'Here is my money."

Mr, Firth counted it. Ten pennies, "This is not even worth one skin. Where did you get it?"

Francis just about cried. If only he could see that white man now!

— *Sarah Simon*

I DIDN'T see money until long after the First World War. The mountain people used to go to Mayo and Dawson in the Yukon to trade their fur. The trader said, "I'll pay you for it," and gave them money.

"He's giving us buttons for our coats!" they said. They didn't like it. When they got to Fort Norman in the springtime they showed it to the people. They were so surprised. Nobody knew what to do with it.

The Bay manager said, "It's worth these many skins."

They never said dollars, they always said skins.

After 1920, white people were working up here and then we started to see dollars.

— *John Blondin*

Nich'it kat duuyeh digitiʔ ahʔok nugadidal. Zheh gwich'o[illegible] geeghee zrih t'igiinch'uh. Zhehk'oo neekat gwizhit t'igiinch'u[illegible] gwitl'at gwijuuk'inʔ. Agwank'oh ts'aii nich'it kat t'iinch'u[illegible] Kwanʔ ehdid ts'aii chan chaa t'iinch'uh, vitiʔ gehghee dhidi[illegible] Gihdiniivyaa, dahant eghee anchaahaahak. Chaa chan ditiʔ eghe[illegible] gihdiniivyaa iiʔan chaataahak. Ako ts'ants'at chaa, nich'id ha[illegible] niłiginaaʔih kwah. Nich'it, chaa hah duuyeh anjoo kat ts'at khugidikhik. Khegidaach'uh. Jii t'at Sarah Simon ako dinuh. Nijin chaa vaghaiʔ leii, nidhizrih, gwid chaa nidhizrii kwaa dai[illegible] łoo guunjih kwaa, gwid nijin nidhizrii daiʔ, at'at zrit tr'iinjo[illegible] uunjih. Aii gwik'it shighaiiʔ neekat juutin ts'at tik gwidilii dan goodhiinjik. Jii t'at Jim Sittichinli ako dinuh.

1921 daiʔ shuuʔii vah t'ihch'uh. Oonjit khyah ełdl[illegible] k'adadał. Drin tsal ts'at nugwidadhat drin, shin chan. Khants'[illegible] nugahaatth'ak ts'at gwilii t'igeediʔah. Igidinii, tr'idinii ha

THE FIRST MONEY was in Arctic Red River. The Indian Boys from here used to work for white men who paid them in money.

"What do we want with this piece of paper? We don't want this?"

As they needed clothing, they wanted to be paid in cloth. But the white people were travelling and didn't carry any spare. Instead they gave them $10 each.

"You give this to the Hudson Bay manager and he'll give you something for it."

When they got back to McPherson, they gave it to John Firth. He said, "That's money and it's worth twenty skins." He gave them twenty skins worth of stuff. Before that nobody knew about money, not even silver money.

— *Andrew Kunnizzi*

FUR BUYERS came in from the Yukon and brought cash to buy muskrats, $3.50 a skin. That's the first time the people understood the value of money.

— *Jim Sittichinli*

I WAS staying with my uncle in 1921 when the white trappers came along at Christmas, Easter, and Summertime. They were falling down and acting so silly.

We didn't know then that they were drunk and we were really scared of them. We didn't know anything about liquor.

— *Elizabeth Yakeleya*

SIDEBAR: ABOUT "FAMILY LIFE" CHAPTER

BEFORE CONTACT (with white people) Dene People lived almost exclusively in the bush and were always on the move, following the migrating herds of caribou. The seasons dictated the pattern of their way of life.

Winter is long with dark days of freezing cold temperatures. Everyone is engaged in relentless and time-consuming hunting for food. After the contact period Dene People also trapped animals for fur during the winter.

In one Dene language, May is called 'the month when you tuck your mittens in your belt'. This is the start of spring, when the rivers run again. People hunted muskrats and beaver for food and fur, went duck and geese hunting, and fished then dried the catch for leaner times.

Summer is hot with days of endless light. Mosquitoes and blackflies swarm. The people go to the fort to trade and meet together. They fish and build canoes, make baskets and nets, tan hides and make clothes, decorating them with moose hair tufting and porcupine quills.

Fall begins in late August and marks the time when the people start back to the hunting grounds. They travel with one or two pack dogs but after contact, had enough extra food to keep a team of dogs to pull the toboggan. They fish until the ice is too thick and then begin to hunt all through the winter again.

– *Sarah Stewart*

3. *Family Life*

Aii guuzhik zrit Hudson Bay tthak nahgwidintl'oh, jidii gwits'an giłtsaii eenjit. Aii tl'ee gwindoo tr'igooheekat eenjit. Jii t'at Andrew Kunnizzi ako dinuh.

"Life in the bush was hard but it sure was a good life. The people were so happy."

— *Andrew Kunnizzi*

Nijin nich'it gwitat t'iinch'uu dahant, diti› hah voondee dinjik dhahkhyaii, dinjik dhoh yits'an ahtsii. Nits'oo adhoh dahah›aa gahdandaii, vighaii› gwits'at tr'iinlii, tl'ee chan dayahchoh ts'at sriinii›aii dant gaih. Vadzaih dhoh tl'il eenjit nizii gahdandaii. Tl'il chan ahtsii. Viti› chan aih ahtsii. Dahant uudahkat, aih hee›at eenjit vahant gayuunahtan tl'ee t'at aih ghat. Jii t'at Elizabeth Yakeleya ako dinuh.

Dugwideedaghan niint'aii gwiinli›. Neekat juutin agwahtshii ts'at yeenoo dai› zhehk'oo dant diiyuundee, diijuu› duuyeh diinin› niłitr'inaa›ih, nihdii tr'igiinkhii. Łeet'ehdehdeelaa chan guunlih. Jii t'at Joe Blondin ako dinuh.

Vahn dai› shitsii khatshiida›uk, aii ts'at shiti› khatshiinda›aih, ahnuh. Charlie, Khatshiinda›aih, yahnuh. Dagoo dathachik yahnuh ts'at deek'it gwits'at khant khatshiinda›aih. Shiti› khant nahdahał , aii ts'at muzzleloader ahchak ts'at chichiłgik. Aii tl'ee dagoo uudahk'ee. Vahant, viti› hah khatshigeeda›ah gwitshih nugwidjiik'ii, goozhik shitsii yinah›ii. Didinjii› tthak zhuudahdhan. Guuti› nin dhoh tthak gwiizii tr'ooheekat gohtsii, diik'ee, chivyah vit'ii onohjii, guugahnuu. Aii chaa kat guughaii› leii tl'ee, tthan› gwadal

HALF of our people lived on the other side of the Mountains and half lived in the Delta, fishing and trapping. After freeze-up, they travelled to the Mountains by dog team. A big family would have two teams with five dogs in each. They travelled from November to late in May then they came together at the head of the Peel.

— Sarah Simon

IT was too late to go back to the trading post then, so they hunted moose to make a mooseskin boat. It's good moose country up there. The men cut good timber and lashed it together with babiche for the frame.

— Jim Sittichinli

THE women took the hair off the moose skins and fleshed it a little bit and sewed it while it was wet. That was for the boat cover. The biggest boat they made was fourteen moose skins.

— Sarah Simon

I SAW them landing in Fort McPherson with five or six families and their dogs. About four days later the men took the boats apart and the women had to clean the skins.

— Sarah Simon

THEY made four boats. They had six oars and six rowers. Smaller boats had four oars and four rowers. You had to keep the boat in the current with the oars and the rest of the time you just let them drop.

— Jim Sittichinli

People at Fort Resolution (Deninu Kué), 1927.
Photo: Public Archives Canada.

Sahtú wife of Bear Lake Chief, with baby.
Photo: National Museums Canada.

Fancy beadwork.
Photo: Frame from the film We Remember.

giheeda?aa goonjii.

1915 aii ts'at 1921 gwits'at school iidi?. Aii tl'ee shuu?ii veenjit k'aniadik. Gwiinzii shits'at giinkhii. Nahant, niti? hah guukwaa, gwid gwiinzii nik'ahaniatiaa. Jidii niidhan, akoo dijiinuh. Nijin teechik goo?aii dant, ezhik vah t'ihch'uh. Aii gwits'at han gwideetoh nandaakaih. Ezhik zheh goodlii gwinaa?ih. Ihłak shiti? vizheh. Ezhit zheh gwihuu shikaiitrii? tsal gajiinlii. Shigii kat chiitee tr'iinlii gugoontrii. Ihłogwinli? zrih iidalii. Niłinaa?ih dant, gwiintl'oh iidatreh. Aii tl'ee shuu?ii vah ehdii tat t'ihch'uh. Khyah chan ts'at gyah ts'at niłzrii hah gahshindaii. Khaii ihłogwinli? vah t'iich'uh. Aii tl'ee 1925 shitr'oonjik. Shidinjii gwiinzii khyah dhidlii, łoo diinjihzhit kwah. Tr'iinjoo chan khyah guudlii.

Shuuri? Elizabeth Yakaleya ts'at shighaii? 72 dilii. Wells dant shigoonlih. Shitsii, shuu?ii, sheek'aii kah hah ezhik t'igiinch'uh. Geetak Fort Norman ninaiididal, itjiich'ii tagwahaandal eenjit. Shin dant, Fort k'aiidadal. 1915 shitsii vakwah. Ezhik shitsii vakwaa dant shighaii? 7 gwidilii. Ihłogwinli? iidalii, shuundee, sheejii kah hah. Aii kat adai?hee Provindence School t'igiinch'u?. Nakhwo lak gugoonlih. Aii

Women's Work

WE didn't hunt caribou but we did lots of trapping. We knew how to set traps for mink and marten. Packing our baby on our back and carrying our packsack, axe, bait, trap — everything. We did our own sewing, cooking and we knew how to cut meat, chop wood and set up tents. We worked really hard. One thing that the women didn't do was go around with their husbands. The women and men stayed very much on their own. The women believed that their duty was to stay home and work.

The men are all decorated up with beads or silk or porcupine quill work. We sew for our husbands and not for ourselves. The women didn't dare put fancy moccasins on. Grandmothers always told us, "Be humble. Remember that woman is not above her husband."

— Sarah Simon

Boys and Girls

WHEN a boy was about ten years old, he went with his dad and learnt to hunt caribou and moose, how to set rabbit snares, fish and trap. If a boy's father wanted him to do well, he started teaching him early.

As soon as the girls could work, their mothers taught them how to tan skins, sew and cook. There were people watching all the time. If she didn't want to learn she would not get a husband. Nobody wants a lazy girl.

— Andrew Kunnizzi

A YOUNG girl dared not go out of her father's sight. She stayed around the tipi. There were always two families, one on one side of the fire and one on the other. The girl sat close to the main entrance and the boy sat on the other side of his father. There was a little doorway by him. The girl always went out of the door on her mother's side and the boy by the other door so that they never met.

— Sarah Simon

guugaʔ shihant, Fort Smith gwits'ee chidhizhih. Nahgwan chan Provindence School gwits'at chidhiidaʔoh, azhik diik'iidhat. T'ehee nakhwoginjik zhit gindakhii. Shuuʔii, oonjit k'it nakhwats'at giinkhii. French chan aii ts'at aachin k'yuuʔ. Aachin k'it vits'at gindakhii. Gwiinzii aachin k'yuu ginohkhii nakhwahnuh.

Adhoh ełshii chan gahshindaii. łuk hah dhihʔaii tthak gahshindaii. Laaswee, naagaii, ch'oo hah k'adiniłkaiʔ. Tr'iinin ihłohjuutin ts'at neekaii iidaʔiʔ. Elizabeth Yakaleya.

1901 ehdii tat shigoonlih. Diik'iishit gwinoo, tr'igiinkhii neenihdik ts'at gaʔoonaatan zheh neeniindik, shitr'ahnuh. Atr'aadzoo gwinahʔih kwaa, k'eʔdinaakaiiʔ, vakaʔaach'uu, ts'at k'eeʔahtraa gahshatr'oonahtan. Nehkak gał chan ts'at nehkak choo, chiitaii gwaʔan tsiidiʔih. Shuh hah atr'aadzoh kwah. Juk gweendoo k'eejit kat aachin adzoo hah agadzoo. Shighaiiʔ nihk'iitik gwidilii dant, mission School gwits'at chidhiizhih. Gashatr'oonahtan gati'iinihdhan, juk drin gwits'at. Aii gwiiyeendoo sheenjit gwiinzii goonlih. Shitsuu diik'ehshandhat. Zheh gwizrih t'iidaach'uh. Shiyoʔghwon kat Hudson Bay chaa giinlih. Shaghaiiʔ vanchohnak'oo zugdhitin ihłii ezhik dant

Boys and girls never answered their Elders back. They had to be very quiet.

— *Sarah Simon*

When a boy was old enough to marry but didn't go out and hunt, but just lay around then he wouldn't get a home as soon as the boy who did go hunting. That's why I didn't get my wife until I was twenty-three!

— *Jim Sittichinli*

When a girl went in the bush with her family her brother would kill a moose and give her the raw hide. She knew how to work at it, how to cut the hair and flesh it, how to hang it to the sun to dry. She knew which caribou hide was good for a dog whip. She took it, tanned it white, then cut it into strips and made it.

When her father made snowshoes, he would make the frame. She would ask her mother how to make babiche and when her mother had shown her she would lace the snowshoes.

— *Elizabeth Yakeleya*

In the morning, about 5:00 or 6:00, my grandfather would catch hold of my father's hand and say, "Charlie, get up! Ptarmigan call for you!" And he'd pull him out of bed.

My father was very light on his feet and he would just jump at the door, take his muzzleloader and run out. He'd go around at daybreak and shoot ptarmigan. Even before anyone else was up, he'd get the ptarmigan ready. Then he'd light the fire.

My grandfather would be watching what he was doing all the time. He would do this with all his sons. The fathers told the boys, "Sell your fur for a good price and buy yourself a gun and a fish net." As soon as the boy is old enough, he tries to collect these things so he owns something.

— *Sarah Simon*

Dry meat and drum, Mackenzie Mountains.
Photo: Bill Stewart.

Camp on riverbank near Fort Good Hope.
National Photography Collection Public Archives Canada.

L-R, son of Bernappee, and mountain men Philip, son of Yennapeee, and St. Pierre who HBC made chief. Fort Good Hope Gwich'in.

Photo: J. Keele 1905, National Museums of Canada.

Snowshoe making.

Photo: Frame from the film We Remember.

shitsuu gwilee vindee kwaa. Aii gwits'at vik'aniłtih. Ch'anuh zhit diik'ashandhat. Niizhuk khaii gwiinleii vik'aniłtii, łoo viłatchidhiizhih kwah. Shitiʔ niveh t'ahʔii kak eenjit gwitr'it t'ugwahʔii. Aklavik dant, shooʔii ookat zheh gwidiʔih. Shooʔii John Firth vik'it. Guutr'iinin kat hah diik'ihshit, shitsuu vik'iigheʔ gwiinleii gugoontrii gwiniłʔih. Sarah Simon.

Tr'iinin kat anjoo goodhiłch'eii. Shinaghan, zheh gwadhoh gwizhit gidii. Gwitr'it tl'ee diiyah gwanduk. Nits'oo tr'igweheendaii eenjit. William Firth vanałdaih. Khahts'at hee shitsuu hah dhidih, shah gwanduk yahnuh. Yahcheedanduk, guuzhik haniidoo ahtsii, k'eʔjahkaiiʔ, guuzhik yahnigwiiʔaih. Akoʔ, William, ezhik sheeghee chidhant'aii, nay gwahałduk, yahnuh. Yeghee chiłt'aii gaa shoh nilih. William gwiinzii shoodhadhanch'aii, nuh. Diik'iindhat jiʔ, chivyaa, gyah, dhuutsah, daaʔaii, diik'ee, aii kat ninints'at kak gwidiniintl'oh, yahnuh. Ahaʔ, shitsuu t'at gwidinidhihtl'oh. Sarah Simon.

Anjoo kat gwiinzii gwihiidindaii geenjit nakhwots'at gigiinkhih. Nijin yeʔeenoo daiʔ gugugwanduk. Sarah Simon.

Adaiʔ gwinoo, diitsuu, diitsii kah hah gwiintl'oh guutr'oodhahch'aii. School giidiłdii k'it t'ugoonch'uh eenjit

Growing Up

My name is Elizabeth Yakeleya and I am 72 years old. I was born in the Wells. My grandfather, father, uncles and aunts all lived there. Once in a while we went to Fort Norman to get supplies.

When we came to the Fort in the summer of 1915 my father died in an accident. I was seven years old. There were five of us children, my brother and sister were already in Providence School. Even though we had relatives near us, my mother could not feed us. She had to go back to Fort Smith to work for the Sisters and we were sent to Providence School. I was raised there.

We still kept our language. My uncle spoke English but we spoke in Slavey to him so he could understand better. He said we spoke well. We had three languages, English, French and Slavey.

I was in school from 1915 until 1921 and then I came back to my uncle. He spoke to me nicely and said, "You are an orphan now, but we'll try our best for you."

I used to think about my parents. My uncle said, "If you wish for anything, just ask."

He took me back to the creek where we used to live. We had left stuff in our houses. We paddled across the river and found the seven houses were still there. I went into my dad's house. My little shoes were still hanging on the wall.

It is terrible to be an orphan, my children. There were only the five of us. We sure cried a lot when we saw each other.

I went in the bush with my uncle and I learn how to trap and hunt and set snares. I stayed with him for five years and then I married in 1925. My husband was a good trapper and I never wanted for anything.

Women used to trap too. I also knew how to tan hides, how to fish, how to sew silk and do bead work and quill sewing. We had twelve children.

— Elizabeth Yakeleya

nits'oo gweheendaii akoo digwinuu. Jim Sittichinli.

Shitsii nakhwah gwanduk. Akoo dinuh. Yeendoo tthak geenjit nakhwa gwilduk. Shagwanduk, nakhwocheet'at zhit dhohʔaii, uuʔan t'ohłih kwah. Ganaondeh shroʔ. Elizabeth Yakelaya.

Nakhwa anjoo diits'at gindakhik kwah. Akoo danaghwagahnuu jiʔ, nihkaa niizhit gwits'at tohjaa gwik'it t'indiʔih. Akoo t'iidiʔih. łaii kwah, tr'eeʔal ts'at diikhah ontshuh tr'achyah. Khyah chan ts'at diik'ee hah tr'eeghah. John Blondin.

Shaghaiiʔ ihłak juutin ts'at neekaii ihłih guuzhik shitiʔ kwah. Shaghaiiʔ vanchohnak'oo zugdhitin ihłih guuzhik chan shahant vakwah. Shitsuu diik'ishandhat. Geetak itjiich'ii iidaʔih kwah. Nakwagehʔat zheh gwadhoh niinʔee gwits'at tahak. Łuhch'uh tsal, vadzaih nilii, dinjik nilii, aii hah sheenjit k'anahtih. Gweeʔee naheedidaa nuudhilʔih. Zheh gwidhoh zhit nihdanahadik, dlok niidhiiʔaih. Isadore Yukon.

Tr'igoonjii. Chaa gwiizii nidhiizrii, khyah chan dhidlii, nich'it vitiʔ yinahʔih. Dinjii gadhidii nizii, vichiʔ oonjii uunuh. Andrew Kunnizzi.

THEY had very strict laws that were twenty times stronger than they are today about how to handle themselves in the family traditions. You couldn't look your mother or sister in the face and answer her back.

Due to respect for one another, brothers and sisters could not talk together. They had to go through an interpreter. It was completely taboo.

— Joe Blondin

I WAS born in the Delta in 1901. When I was growing up we were told to go to church and go to school. We never went to a dance or anything. There was nothing like that then.

We learnt how to sew, cook and wash. We used to play bat and ball, football, just children's games out of doors. We didn't have drum dancing. The young people do it now but they picked it up from the Slavey.

I went to the mission day school when I was six years old. From that time on and still today I am interested in learning. My school days were the best time of my life.

My grandmother brought me up and I stayed in town because my family were Hudson Bay people. When I was nine years old my grandmother lost her sight and I had to look after her. She had brought me up very carefully in the Christian way. Now for nine years I had to look after her. There was not even one time that I left her.

My father was working for the police in Aklavik, my uncles had their stores, like my uncle John Firth. Most of the time I was brought up with their children because of my grandmother. But still I had a hard time.

— Sarah Simon

K'asho Got'ine Sahtú Boy at Fort Good Hope (K'asho Got'ine).
Photo: National Museum of Canada.

Old Steamboat,' Gwich'in man, making a fishnet in Old Crow (Teechik).
Photo: National Museums of Canada.

Dinjii k'eejit nizii goonlih jiʔ, tr'iinjoo dahɫeii vishiʔih niidha akoo daheedach'ah. Tr'iinjoo chan veenjit akoo t'ugoonch'u Tr'iinjoo vigwidjantl'oo nilii jiʔ, duulee dinjii ihɫak unts'at h diʔih. Gwiizii nihts'at t'igidiʔih. Guutr'iinin kat zhehk'oo ihɫa k'it t'igiinch'uh. Jim Sittinchinli.

Hudson Bay Company zhit nigeheedaa gwitshih da gwits'at, dinjii ihɫee dinjii khehkaiʔ nilii. Aii ts'at yinjiʔtr'iɫʔe Adant zrih, danuu vak'agwaadhat. Hudson Bay kat chan dinj khehkaiʔ danuu guudhiɫch'aii. Ezhit gwanoo t'aii hee yeʔeen daiʔ gwidinjii k'it gugwindaii.

Guutat t'ehee geetak aghan gahtsii. Dinjii khehkaiʔ zrih guuts' giinkhih. Akwaa nuh daiʔ, gwik'it t'ugoonch'uh. Dinjii khehka vakwaa tl'ee vidinjiiʔ ihɫee goo guuvilak ihɫee giideek'it guunji Nihzhuu naditjii, tthak zhuu diʔih. Chief Julius aii datr'oonji vitsii dinjii khehkaiʔ iinliʔ. Dinjii niint'aii nilii, viginjik niint'a nilii. Sarah Simon.

Chief Julius dinjii niint'aii iinliʔ. Hudson Bay dinj khehkaiʔ eenjit nilii. Dinjii gwiinzii nidhizrii, khyah ch dhidlii. Dinjii tthak yinjiʔgichiɫʔeh. Tthak tr'oodhahch'a Johnny Kaye.

Hand Games at Fort Good Hope, 1927.
Photo: National Photography Collection Public Archives Canada.

The Role of the Elders

THE children were taught to listen to their Elders. The old women used to sit around in the corner of the tent after all the work was done and there was nothing else to do. Then it was, "Grandma, tell us a story."

So she would tell them a story about how to live.

I remember William Firth used to come every evening and say to my grandmother, "Tell me a story!"

She got fed up with him because she was making sinews and sewing and he was bothering her, so she said, "Alright, William, lie down here beside me and I will tell you a story."

He was glad and lay down beside her.

"William listen to me good. When you grow up make sure you have a net, snares, a chisel, an axe and a good gun. Five things. Did you write it on your forehead?"

"Oh sure grandmother. I wrote it."

— *Sarah Simon*

Mrs. Lazarus and baby, Old Crow (Teechik).
Photo: Yukon Public Archives.

Sahtú boy in his hare skin parka.
Photo: Public Archives Canada.

THE grandchildren look to the old people very much. They are more like a school for them, putting them to school in their way of life.

— Jim Sittichinli

WHEN my grandfather told us a story he would say, "I am telling you this not only for these days but for the future. Take my words and don't throw them away. Put them in your pocket and keep them always."

— Elizabeth Yakeleya

WE never talked back to our Elders. If they said, "Tomorrow you are going 50 miles away," you did it. You didn't have a dog team, you walked and carried your packsack, traps and muzzle-loader with you.

— John Blondin

I WAS ten or twelve when my father died. My mother died when I was nine. So my grandmother brought me up on nothing. We didn't have a thing. She would go to the next tent and get a piece of bannock or some caribou or moose meat for me, whatever she could, and she'd save it for me. I waited for her to come back and when she came into the tent, I smiled.

— Isadore Yukon

Marriage

IF there was a very good young man, he was entitled to have as many wives as he wanted. It was the same with women. If there was a very smart woman, she could have more than one husband.

They would treat each other well and their children were just like one family.

— Jim Sittichinli

EVEN before Hudson Bay Company came here the Loucheux always had one man for chief and advisor. He was the head

Johnny Kay chan dinjii khehkaiʔ nizii iinliʔ. Peter Thompson.

Adaiʔ gwinoo dinjii lat kat ddhah tat gwich'in ts'at guulat chan k'aii van gwich'in giinlih. Dinjii khehkaiʔ gidiʔih, dinjii tih chan vahjaa. Aii kat vah tshid giinlih. Shik ediiyeetshih gugwinahʔin. Łoo tr'iguudinjik guunlih kwah. Tsee agwahntshii nihgehdeedindee, khaii gwiiyeet'iiʔ. Joe Blondin.

Nijin Norman, Good Hope gwits'at katr'idadal, gwiinzii guuts'at t'igwidiʔih. Gwiinleii dinjii zhuh, aachin kahah nikhah nugahdadal, aii geenjit adaiʔ gwinoo ganagwandaii. Daang ts'at ihłogwinliʔ nihzhuu nadijii. Tthak nihłinehch'iʔ dinjii nilii. Sarah Simon.

Aii ts'at dinjii kat han gwidiʔ chuu vee gwaʔan, dinjii zhuh, eneekaii kah hah gwiinzii nihts'at t'igidiʔih. Gwit'ih tr'agwahtsii ganangiiʔjiʔ gwadhat kwah. Dinjii zhuh kat zrit akoo digiinch'uh. Jim Sittichinli.

of the people and they respected him. He was the only one who could give advice. They went to him for everything and did what he said. The Hudson Bay really depended on the chief. When the chief died one of his sons or his nearest relatives took his place from generation to generation.

Chief Julius (Salu) was chosen because his grandfather was chief. He was a strong person and didn't talk much but his voice had great power.

— Sarah Simon

CHIEF JULIUS was a strong powerful man. He was the Hudson Bay Chief and the Band Chief. He was a good hunter and trapper and his people respected him. Everyone listened to him.

— Johnny Kaye

Johnny Kaye... he was a good chief.

— Peter Thompson

The people in the old days had communities by themselves, like the Mountain Indians and the Willow Lake Tribe. They had a band leader with three or four sub-chiefs under him, who acted as a council. They were always looking ahead. There was not a lazy bone in one. They were like beavers and had to do their share for the coming winter.

— Joe Blondin

WHOEVER came down from Norman or Good Hope was always treated well by us. Lots of times the Loucheux and Slavey moved around together. That's why, if you trace back four or five generations, you'll find the different tribes are all related.

— Sarah Simon

IF the people travelled up the river or down the coast among other Indians or among the Eskimo, they always treated each other well. They never charged each other anything. That's the Native way.

— Jim Sittichinli

SIDEBAR: ABOUT "BOAT TIME" CHAPTER

In 1885 the first steamer in the Northwest Territories, SS ***Wrigley*** was built at Fort Smith. She and her sister ships SS ***Mackenzie*** and SS ***Distributor*** sailed down the Mackenzie River to the Arctic Ocean each summer taking supplies to all the forts.

– *Sarah Stewart*

4. Boat Time

"Everyone really waited for it and when I saw it,
I thought it was the most wonderful thing that
I had ever seen."

— Sarah Simon

Ganałdaih, tr'ih choo nitshii alah daiʔ, too gwitanaanch'uu, chaa, nich'it ka hah, gadhaondaii, ts'at tr'ih choo khaodooʔih, guutr'ahnuh. Tthak ts'at chan k'ehtr'ajahkaiʔ ts'at tr'iilee tr'igwahtsii. Tr'ih choo, nugwidadhat ihłak gwizrih nanadilak. Geenjit shoh giinlih. Tr'aʔaa tanahtr'aazhik. Giikhii choo chan yizhit k'aheedik. Dhaachuh guuzhik tr'ih choo alaa, hah tr'azral. Aii ts'at khatshiitr'aazhik. Diigwich'aa nizii natr'aazhii. Nagal tr'ahaadal, diizheh gwadhoh zhit gwiinzii tr'igwahtsii. Datchanchyah k'eegahtrah ts'at gihłiʔjiidatan chan aachin kat k'adadal diizheh nigitjah. Han iidiʔ tr'igwinahʔii, yeʔeediʔ niinzhit łat nitshii tr'anahʔii. Ts'at tl'eedik nitr'ijilzhih gwihdahtr'ijaa, teevee gwits'at tr'ih choo tik gwidilih ts'at zral. Dinehtl'eh chan k'alik. Giikhii choo chan, dinjii, tr'iinjoo ka hah giidijuujaa. Aii tl'ee chan dinjii kat khahgoo ghwohłii, niizhit iichuu guhgwehehlii.

Drin daang tthak tr'ih choo dhitin. Aii tl'ee tr'ih choo nachidhilit. Dinjii khehkaiʔ ookat zheh, Hudson Bay, aanaii giiyahnuh. Łuh gah itjiich'ii leii giits'an ahtsii, laavaasdaa eenjit. Guutat shrah daatrak, tthak ts'at gwiʔee tohjah. Chaa, nich'it ka hah giits'at tahuk. Shitr'iinjoo, adaiʔ hee nilii gaii chuu

SS Distributor leaving Fort Good Hope, 1924.
Photo: Louis Romanet Collection The University of Alberta Archives.

John Firth told the People that a big boat would be coming in July, and that it ran by burning wood. Everyone really waited for it and when I saw it, I thought it was the most wonderful thing that I had ever seen.

I remember when the steamer Mackenzie used to come. Every night the boys and girls are told, "Stay up and watch for the boat coming."

Everyone is sewing and getting ready for the arrival.

The boat only comes once a year, so we are excited. It means we will have groceries and also our bishop will be coming. While we are sleeping we hear somebody shouting, "Steamboat! Steamboat!"

We get out of bed and put on our best new clothes and then we all run around cleaning up the inside of the tents, tidying around the doorway, washing our floors and sweeping. Tourists will be coming into our homes.

You can see twelve miles down the stretch of the river and so we can see the smoke in the distance. When it's coming closer, we stand on the top of the bank or climb down to the shore.

zhidhidlii, laavaasdaa eenjit. Dinjii nitshii nilii, viginjik niint'aii. Chaa kat chuu guunjih, troo chan guunjih. Kwanɂ deek'it gwiintshii gugwahtsih, nilii, łuk hah łuh ch'uh vakagahch'uh. Chaa ihłee łuhch'uh ahtsih. Esau George vaazhii.

Kwantat gwaɂan łuh vizhit vakatr'ahch'uu tahwahjii. Ganałdaii, tr'idinii, chaa, nich'id ka hah gazral. Ihłee ga łoo idinii ganinjiɂahdhat kwah. Ts'at gwiizuu gwahtsii kwah. Shoh giinlih ts'at nikhah gwitr'it t'ugwahɂii. Tl'oo nizii kat neɂginiinlih. Tr'iinjoo kat agwank'oh ts'aii gijilch'eii. Tr'iinin kat chan guuveenjit dhok gahdaach'aa sritr'igwiniinlii. Chaa, nich'it ka hah shih guutat gilih. Giikhii ihłee naaɂeh ts'at shih k'oo giikhih. Aii tl'ee tthak ts'at ch'ik zhit shih leii hah gwaɂan nahtr'ijah. Dinjii khehkaiɂ diitat ts'at giikhii gah dinjii kat mahsiɂ ginuu.

Dinjii khehkaiɂ ooɂan neeghwotjah, tl'ee zheh gwiintshii gwits'at tr'iheedah. Tthak ts'at gwiizii neetr'aagwaazhii. Aii ts'at tr'igiinkhii gwiinzii tr'igwahtsii.

Hudson Bay, khaii eenjit itjiich'ii diits'an gahtsii. Aii tl'ee chan atr'aadzoo. Dinjii khehkaiɂ tthak ts'at oodzoo guugahnuh. Shinaghan kat shuɂ oodzoo jiɂ, nakhwo ginɂ datchanchyah kat nahtohghwogoh. William Firth gwiizii iitsii edlii adahłii. Jim ts'at Joseph Greenland gwiizii agaadzoo. K'eejit kah chan nihts'at agaadzoh. Gwiintl'oh srugoonch'uu gugwahtsii. Sarah Simon.

The steamer whistles three times. That means it's bringing mail. When it docks we meet the bishop. Then, men and women pack freight up the steep hill on their backs.

The boat is here for four or five days. After it leaves the Chief is asked to come to the store and Hudson Bay give him a 50-pound bag of flour and everything he needs for the feast. He shouts, "All you people with boys and girls send them here to me! My wife is soaking drymeat for the feast!" He is a big man and has a big voice.

The boys haul water and bring up driftwood or dry willows and make a great long place for the fire. They build a fire and boil meat or fish. The best bannock maker is one of the boys. His name is Esau George. He mixes the bannock then gathers all the frying pans in the settlement. I remember that real nice brown bannock in the frying pan.

"Drink tea! Drink tea!" the boys and girls are shouting. Nobody ever thinks of drinking alcohol or wants to disturb the peace. They are just happy working together.

They set places on the dry clean grass. The women sit on one side, the men on the other side, in long rows. There is one place for the children.

The boys and girls serve, just like a potluck supper. One of the churchmen stands up and says grace and we eat. After we finish everybody gets a big dish full of food to take home. Then the Chief gives a speech and one of the other men gets up and gives thanks. Then everybody thanks the Chief.

The last thing he says is, "Take your food and dishes home then come back to the community hall."

Everybody gets dressed up and we attend our big service. Hudson Bay now gives us our Hudson Bay winter supplies. Then we have our dance. The Chief says, "Everybody is to come. Old women who cannot dance use your elbows and crawl on the floor!"

William Firth is at the fiddle, Jim and Joseph Greenland are good dancers. The young people get up and jig. We just have a good time.

— Sarah Simon

Packing goods and fur at Fort Resolution, Great Slave Lake.
Photo: Provincial Archives of Alberta, E. Brown Collection.

Dene camp on Mackenzie River with steamboat in the background.
Photo: Louis Romanet Collection University of Alberta Archives.

Great Bear Lake dant, Hudson Bay ezhit kwah. Fort Norman tthak ts'at gwits'ee tr'eedah. Ezhik tr'ih choo nitshii tahnahdahlak. K'aii Van gwich'in kat, Ddhah Tat gwich'in kat, Wrigley gwits'at, Good Hope gwits'at. Tthak nihts'at tr'ahaadal. Aii kaii k'it gwizhit tsiiʔin, tthak ts'at tsiitr'idiʔii. Dinjik tth'anʔ hah chan tsiitr'idiʔii. Iitsii edlii hah atr'aadzoo, tl'ee tr'ih choo nahdahlak. Nijin K'aii Han gwinjik niłahaniaʔyiaa eenjit t'ijiidinuh. Elizabeth Yakeleya.

1926 gwinoo tr'ih choo Teetl'it Zheh taadhidlit. Ligis zhit oranges aii chan tatr'oodlii. Hudson Bay kat gwitahgiiyilii. Dinjii ts'at ihłak 25 cent dilii. Orange nak'oh zrih diits'an tr'ahtsii. Gwiinzii vagwandaii. Vakwaa jiʔ, gat'iinihdhan kwah, aii ts'at niizhuk shaadhiliah. Aii at'at nugwidadhat ihłak geenjit. Jim Sittichinli.

Oonjit zhii gweendoo at'iinihdhan. Aii gwiiyeendoo vat'iinihdhan, łuhch'uh luʔ. Aii sheenjit shih nizii. Shitiʔ valak kat aanaii giiyahnuu, vahchidhiizhih. (Nijin gwaʔan nahadik, vah natshihdik). Valak iitsii tyah diʔgehniint'uh, nichih tloo nilih, dhandaii oojihnuh. Ch'ik tsal zhit vilat k'eʔgwiłʔaih, łoo dhandaih kwah. Dinjii kat gwiiyeendo łoo giiyuukat kwah. Ihłak ts'at neekaii agwahntshii zrih. Andrew Kunnizzi.

THERE was no Hudson Bay on Great Bear Lake at that time, so everybody went into Fort Norman when the steamboat was coming. There the Willow Lakers, the Caribou Point people, Mountain people and people from Wrigley and from Good Hope came together. We sure enjoyed ourselves in town. We played hand games, moose bone games, and had a fiddle dance. After the steamer had gone, we set a date when we would meet again at the mouth of the Willow River.

— Elizabeth Yakeleya

THE boat that came in 1926 to Fort McPherson brought a few cases of oranges. Hudson Bay used to divide the oranges between the people. They cost 25 cents each and you only got a quarter of an orange! It tasted so good. I didn't like to see it go so I just sucked it to make it last. And that was the finish for another year.

— Jim Sittichinli

THE white man's food I liked best was hardtack. That was a very good food for me. One time my father was invited to his friend's and I went too. (I followed him everywhere.) This friend opened a can of tomatoes. I thought they would be sweet and I tasted them with a spoon. They weren't sweet at all! The people never bought much food at all. Just one or two cans to take back in the bush.

— Andrew Kunnizzi

Denehtl'eh nugwidadhat gwizhit neekat natr'anahɔik. Dinjii neekant kat Good Hope gwits'at denehtl'eh k'anugidizoh. Dachaavał ts'ał geeliɫ. Guu zhii ts'at denehtl'eh hah gwizhit guudlih. Aii tl'ee denehtl'eh hah k'agidaɔoh. Tl'ee shin chan denehtl'eh tr'ih choo zhit k'atriiik. Johnny Kaye.

Adaiɔ gwinoo iitsii vizhit tr'igiinkhii tr'uudhilch'eii kwah. ɫaii tl'ah didaach'ee diɔih. Kaii k'it gwits'at chan gahɔat ɫaii tr'ineezhaa ts'at gwits'at tr'ahɔoh. Srii nihk'iitik tl'ee zrit dinehtl'eh tr'inahɔin. Ganaɫdaih, Norman Wells dant denehtl'eh hah katr'idaɔoh. Khyah t'ahɔii, voozriɔ Herbert Hudson vaazhii. Adant chan ts'at George Johnson aii hah geenjit nihdits'at gigiinkhih. Aii yeenjit nankat tseedhoh dugwahntshii dilii jukwaahee denehtl'eh kat gugwanahɔii. Srii nihk'iidaang ako dahshuk gwitshuhdhat. Joe Blondin.

MAIL used to come in twice a year. Two men used to go for mail up to Fort Good Hope from here. They pulled a little toboggan with their food, bedding and mail up to Fort Good Hope. They brought mail back the same way. Then in the summertime, mail came in by the boat.

— Johnny Kaye

THERE was no radio, no communication. You only received mail once a year. The government had dog teams in every Fort from Waterways all the way down to Tuk.

You loaded your mail on the dog team and went to the next fort where another team was waiting. It took about six months to get an answer to a letter.

I remember one time the mail came to Norman Wells. There was a trapper by the name of Herbert Hudson. He and George Johnson were arguing about the outside prices that they'd just read in the newspaper. It was only eight months old!

— Joe Blondin

SIDEBAR: ABOUT "MISSIONARIES" CHAPTER

The missionaries came to the North with the help of the Hudson's Bay Company. The Oblates of Mary Immaculate arrived in 1845 and in 1866 were joined by the Grey Nuns. Together they built missions and started the schools at Fort Resolution, Fort Providence, and Fort Smith.

By 1920 there was a Roman Catholic mission at every trading post in the Mackenzie Valley except for the Anglican Community of Fort McPherson. Reverend Kirkby, the first Anglican Missionary had arrived there in 1852. By 1903 Edward Sittichinli, Jim Edward Sittichinli's father, was ordained; the first Anglican Gwich'in Minister.

– Sarah Stewart

5. Missionaries

"Some of the missionaries now, when they look back,
they realize they did harm to the People."

— *Mary Wilson*

Giikhii k'eheedadal gwitshih, dinjii kat k'agwaadhat gahgidindaih. Gwiinzii, gwiizuu hah, tr'iinin kat ooghohts'it kwaa agahnuh. Gwiizuu gahgidindaii. Itjiich'ii guuts'an nilii kwaa, guunjik jiʔ, aii gwiizuu gahgidindaii. Anjoo kat k'eejit gwiizii gwitr'it t'agwahʔii kwaa ganahʔii daiʔ, anaa guugahnuh. Tsuh ninahʔih ginuh. Aii ts'at guutr'anahʔii gahgidindaii. Jim Sittichinli.

Shitsuu ako dashahnuh, k'agwaadhat hah gahgweedindaiʔ gwitshih, digitr'iinin akoo dagahnuu, too nugwidjaazhit, nihdeenighoojah, khehdohnuu, tsuk nigwehdeetth'ak. Sarah Simon.

Yeʔeenjiʔ chuu tl'it, chii juuk'anʔ goonlih. Tth'aii ezhit t'iinch'uh. Jidii t'iinch'uu giiyahdindaii kwah. Han duh ts'aii t'igiinch'uh. Gwiintsal niizhit dant. Aii gwits'at łat choo ganahʔih, khaii ts'at shin daiʔ tr'inahʔih. Guuyoʔghwon kat chiitaii tsiighoʔih kwah. Zheh gwizhit t'ohch'uh. Oodhodhohch'eii. Egitjiitth'ak, dinjii tsiiʔin hah tsiidiʔih k'it

BEFORE the missionaries came, we learnt about God and the people already knew there was right and wrong. The Elders taught the young people not to tell lies. They knew it was wrong. They knew if you took something which didn't belong to you that was wrong too.

Every time an older person saw a young person do something wrong the Elder would say, "Don't do that. Marten is looking at you!" They knew God was watching over them.

— Jim Sittichinli

MY Grandmother told me that in the old days, parents would tell their children as soon as it was getting dark, ''Come into the tipi. Stay in and don't make any noise or Marten will hear you."

— Sarah Simon

WAY up the Peel River there were some burning coal seams. They are still there today. They didn't know what the cause of it was in those days. When they set their camps on the other side of the river, quite a way from that place, they could see the big smoke and even flames in winter and in summer.

The parents would say, "Don't play outside. Stay in and listen." They would hear noises that sounded like people were playing games in the flames and other sounds like people crying and really moaning.

My grandmother's mother would tell her, "Go to bed and don't make a noise. The happiness and laughter is good people but the crying is bad people. If you make a noise you will disturb them and you too will go to that place."

— Sarah Simon

Jesus Christ on the cross, hanging in a Catholic Church.
Photo: Frame from the film We Remember.

Praying, 1870.
Photo: Frame from the film We Remember.

School children at the Mission in Hay River, 1925.
Photo: Public Archives Canada.

Oblates at Fort Rae, 1924.
Photo: Public Frame from the film We Remember, Public Archives Canada.

t'igwinuh, tr'itreh k'it chan t'igwinuh. Shitsuu akoo shihanh dahnuh, dhiintshih, gajaantth'ak kwah. Shoh goonlii daiʔ, tr'eedlah, aii dinjii niizii t'inuh. Tr'itreh daiʔ, dinjii iizuu t'inuh. Khehdohch'uh kwaa jiʔ, aii gwits'at tiinhah, guuvahnuh. Sarah Simon.

Yeʔeenoo daiʔ dinjii dazhan gwinuu. Dinjii gwik'iijizhit. Giikhii kat aii gwik'it goonlih kwaa ginuh. Ejuk ts'at tr'igwindaii gugwahtsih. Niinzhuk gwitshuudhat tl'ee hee k'agwaadhat hah gahgidindaii. Jim Sittichinli.

Roman Catholic giikhii kat tr'oochit dinjii gaguunahtan. Aii tl'ee ddhah tat ts'at chuuzhih. Archdeacon MacDonald, Anglican Giikhii dinjii zhuh hah gwitr'it t'uguwahʔih. Johnny Kaye.

Shitshih gwanoo hee zhat giikhii gugwanahʔii. Aii gaa gugwaanduk shiʔih. Anglican giikhii, William Kirkby vaazhii. Aii k'agwaadhat gaʔoonahtan. Khaii tik tl'ee hee RC giikhii zhat gwinahʔih. Shitsii, Mr. Firth, shigiikhii ka hah Winnipeg gwits'at k'agidadal. Tsiigehtshik dant k'ii tr'ih zhit k'agidadal. Oonjit kat k'agidadal, dinjii zhuh k'yuu gigiinkhih kwah ts'at k'eejit giinlih. Dinjii zhuh nich'it tahgwigwiljik, digiginjik zhit guuts'at gigiinkhih. Gwiinzii guuginjik ek'eganjik. Hudson Bay dinjii,

In the old days there were people called Medicine People. The people believed in them. The missionaries put a stop to that and showed us a different way to live.

It took a long long time before the people understood the Christian teachings.

— Jim Sittichinli

The Roman Catholic priest came first and taught the people and gave them rosaries. Then he went to the mountains. Archdeacon MacDonald was an Anglican Missionary who worked with the Loucheux.

— Johnny Kaye

The missionaries first came here long before my time but I have the history. The Anglican minister who came here was William Kirkby and he taught the people about the true God. About two or three years before that the Roman Catholic priest had come through.

My grandfather, old Mr. Firth, and my missionary came from Winnipeg to Red River, down the Mackenzie to here in a birchbark canoe. The white men didn't speak Loucheux and they were all very young. They took Native girls to live with them. Soon these girls picked up broken Scottish accents and they taught their husbands Loucheux. So that's how they began to understand each other.

One Hudson Bay man was living with a woman who was later baptized as Mary. She told the people that a man of God would be coming and she really helped the missionary.

— Sarah Simon

We think Christmas is a great day. As soon as we learnt about it from the Hudson Bay and the missionaries, we celebrated it with a church service, feast and a dance.

Not hand games. Our church taught us not to play hand games so the Anglican people don't do that.

The Hudson Bay people and the missionary were all from

tr'iinjoo uunjik, aii Mary vaazhii. Diitat ts'at giinkhii, k'agwaadhat eenjit. K'agwaadhat neeheedaa nuh, ts'at giikhii ts'at tr'iinjih. Sarah Simon.

S.75. Drin tsal, drin nitshii uujiidinuh. Hudson Bay kat, giikhii ka hah guuk'iighe gwik'anaanjik. Tr'igiinkhii gwiintshii tr'igwahtsii. Aii tl'ee laavaatsaa tr'ahtsii. Atr'aadzoh. Uudzii hah tsiigwahii kwah. Nakhwa tr'igiikhii zheh gwizhit akoo danakhwatr'ahnuh. Hudson Bay dinjii, giikhii hah Scotland gwits'at t'igiinch'uh. Drin Choo gahtsii. Nakhwent'eh, Drin Choo aatsih. Aii tl'ee gwinoo, tr'igiikhii zheh gwits'at gwik'anjik. Drin tsal gwiiyeendo drin chiłee nilih. Sarah Simon.

S.76. Zhat nakhwa giikhii, Archdeacon Whittaker, Anglican nilih. Aii akoo dinuu, nichi ts'at aii chaa hah nigooheendal. Nich'it nizii nilii gwiinzii chan k'ehjahkai, vigwitr'it gweheezah. Juu giikhii ts'at dinuu, guuti, guuhant hah geenjit ihłoo gidikhih kwah. Nich'it, chaa yuunjii gat'iiniidhan kwaa guuga. Shint'eh gahshindaii ts'at aii nich'it vahshindaii. Vahant, shitsuu ts'at giikhii, John Firth, Hudson Bay dinjii nilii, gahdandaii, akoo digiihaanjaa yahnuh. Ts'at Mr. Firth akoo diyahnuu, aii chaa needeenyuh nizii heelah. Aii tl'ee gweee shitsuu ts'at

Scotland so they celebrated New Year's Day. That meant we celebrated it too. Later on, we learnt from the church that we should celebrate Christmas as the greatest day.

— Sarah Simon

OUR Anglican minister here, Archdeacon Whittaker, was the one who would say, "Your daughter and that boy are going to get married. She is a good girl, a good worker and can sew and will do well."

When the minister suggested this the parents could do nothing about it even if the girl didn't want to marry the boy. I saw it myself of course and I knew the girl. Her mother came and talked to my Grandmother who told her to go to John Firth, the Hudson Bay Manager. She said he would know what to do.

So the mother went there but Mr. Firth said, "I believe that boy will be a very good son-in-law for you."

So she came back to my Grandmother. "I can't do any more," she said. "Mr. Firth says go ahead. It must be done."

The day the girl married I saw her coming out of the church and she was crying. But what could that help?

— Sarah Simon

I BECAME a woman church member when I was very young. I was very interested in teaching. I often wish I had been trained somewhere but I couldn't leave my grandmother. I had to stay with her all the time until I got married.

My husband could speak but not read English. He could read and write Loucheux. I told him I was going to read to him and teach him. He said, "I'm not a Scotch breed. Just do your book. I want to work outdoors!"

I started to cry. I thought he meant it, but he was just teasing me! I got him very interested in learning English and he began his training for the ministry in 1927. We went back to Hay River School. My husband took Bible lessons and I took music lessons. I played the organ. We were in

Tipi in front of the church at Fort Simpson (Liidli Kue).
Photo: T. Brown Collection.

Bishop Breynat and children at Fort Resolution (Denınu Kue).
Photo: National Photography Collection Public Archives Canada.

Fort Providence (Zhahti Koe) school picnic, 1926.
Photo: Ernestine Burke Collection.

Convent of the Sacred Heart, Fort Providence (Zhahti Koe).
Photo: National Photography Collection Public Archives Canada.

nachiidhizhii, at'at geenjit duuyeh ihłoo t'ishiʔih, yahnuh. Mr. Firth akoo dinuu, gwik'it t'ugweediʔyiaa. Nich'it tr'oonjik, treh ts'at tr'igiikhii zheh gwits'at cheedizhii, gwid geenjit dugweheediʔyiaa. Sarah Simon.

Tr'iinjoo k'eejit ihłih daiʔ, tr'igiikhii zheh gwijaa ihłih. agaonałtan gat'iinihdhan. Geetak iizhii dehk'it gashatr'oonahtan nihdhan gwid duuyeh shitsuu viłachihzhii. Shitr'ooheendal gwits'at. Shidinjiiʔ dinjii zhuh k'yuu giinkhih, gwid oonjit k'yuu giinkhih kwah. Duulee oonjit k'yuu ganuuhanałchah vałnuh. Half breed ihłih kwaa, niedinehtl'eh zrih hah gahdhiinʔaih, shahnuh. Chiitaii gwaʔan gwitr't t'igwiłʔii gwizrih nihdhan, aii ts'at ihtreh. Oonjit k'yuu gavuuniłtan, aii geenjit shoh nilih. 1927 gwits'at giikhii gwitr'it t'igwahʔii. Aii tl'ee Hay River School gwits'at chidhiidaʔoh. Shidinjiiʔ edinehtl'eh choo oonahtanʔ, shiichan organ etr'idlii gashatr'oonałtan. Nugwidadhat neekaii ganakhwatr'oonahtan. Shidinjiiʔ 33 khaii ndooʔ ts'at akoo dahshuk gatr'oonahtan.

Tr'igiihkii gwahtsii, kaii k'it gwizhit gijiinjih. Datchan tat gwaʔan chan dinjii eenjit tr'igiikhii ahtsih. Geeghee ts'at nizrii ts'at kyah t'ahʔii ts'at łuk kadiʔih. Aii nugwidadhat gwiinleii gwitr'it t'ugwahʔii, nakhwatr'ookat kwah. Łuh, 150 lbs. akoo dugwahtshii ts'at tr'aʔaa nakhwots'an gahtsii. Tr'igiikhii zheh gwits'at nugwidadhat 33 akoo dahshuk gwiintl'oh gwitr'it t'ugwahʔih. Aii tl'ee Whitehorse gwits'at chidhiidaʔoh. Ezhit school for two years but training continued for my husband for 33 years.

He took church services and prayers in the town and in the bush. We travelled everywhere with the people. Besides that, we were hunting, trapping and fishing. And all these years we were never paid. I don't like to say it because we never asked for payment. We did have about 150 pounds of flour and a few little things besides. About $200 worth of groceries from the church. So for 33 years we worked hard in the town and in the bush.

We went to Whitehorse. We were asked to work amongst the Indians there. We didn't understand them and they didn't understand us either so the first thing we did was make friends with the old people. As soon as they got to know us, they really liked us.

These poor Indians used to live in Whitehorse and know their church both Roman Catholic and Anglican. Their children went to Carcross School. Whitehorse was their town. But in 1945 the army came through and there were so many white people. They came like mosquitoes.

The Indians were pushed by the riverside to the place called Whiskey Flats. They started losing their young boys and girls, even older people. There was so much drinking going on, they lost their faith, everything.

Then they were put at Moccasin Flats where the old steamer used to be, in old shacks. When they were filled, they were asked to go across the river where it was quiet. Two or three people built there but then they were told to move back. You see how they pushed those Indians around.

Now they are up on an Indian Reserve far away from the Yukon River. While I was there they built a well for them, but it wasn't keeping clean. Shorty Scurvey was the chief then and he really complained about it. I don't know what they gave them. I think it is a poor way to treat the Indians. Week after week we used to visit them in Pelly, dinjii zhuh tat gwitr'it t'igohʔii, nakhwatr'ahnuh. Nakhwoginjik gitjiitth'ak kwah. Nakhwent'eh guujiidatth'ak kwah. Anjoo kat tr'oochit lak guujaa dhaatsaii, gwiintł'oh nakhwa t'igiiniidhan.

Aii dinjii zhuh kat gwitshih daiʔ, Whitehorse t'igiinch'uh. Digitr'igiikhii zheh gah gahdindaii, RC chan ts'at Anglican guugii kat Carcross School t'igiinch'uh. Whitehorse guukaiik'it goonlih gwid 1945 nivehł'ahʔii ezhit k'agidadal. Oonjit kat goonlih, ch'ii k'it łoo t'igiinch'uh. Aii dinjii zhuh kat handuh ts'aii nigootr'iinlih, Whiskey Flat guuvaazhii. Aii gwits'at chan k'eejit nich'it ka hah anjoo gaa gwintł'oh etr'idinii , gwik'iinjigwizhit hah tr'agwedindak. Aii tł'ee Moccassin Flat nigoo tr'iinlii, ezhit tr'ih choo steamer vaazhii ezhit iintinʔ. Zheh googwiłtsaii, tł'ee gehłeeghwotjaa guutr'ahnuh.

Aii tł'ee niizhit gwaʔan t'igiinch'uh. Yukon han gahʔat ezhit t'ihch'uh goozhik nan zhit chuu deek'it guuveenjit tr'agwałtsaii. Gwiinzii guukatr'anahtih kwah. Shorty Scurvey guukhehkaiʔ nilii geenjit gwiintł'oh giinkheh. Dinjii zhuh gwizii ts'at t'igwidiʔih kwah. Pelly, Carmacks, Ross River, Mayo, guuveeneeniidadal. Taii tr'igwahtsii gwitr'it goonlii. Dinjii zhuh kat tseedhoh leii gałtsaii. Itr'idinii hah guutseedhoh kwah.

Young Sarah Simon with Rev. James Simon and children Charlie and Susie.

Carmacks, Ross River and Mayo. When the highway came through there was lots of work. The Indians made lots of money but it all went on booze. The Government built houses for them, but couldn't they have built their own?

Once they were put there what can they do on the Reserve? There was a Roman Catholic church there and a Baptist church and that was all.

They used to walk down to Whitehorse every morning. They've got no place to go. They go to the bars. It's not their fault that they're drinking. They didn't make it for themselves. Many times I saw them with no place to go. It was too far to go home.

For 33 years we worked really hard, then all at once my husband was called from Whitehorse by Bishop Greenwood. He just jumped up. He never even sat down

Tshid nilii guuveenjit zheh gugwałtsaii. Aii tl'ee kheenjit ihło t'igiheediʔyiaa kwah. Ezhit RC tr'igiikhii zheh gooʔaii. Bapti: chan aii gwizrih nugahdadal.

Vanh gwitugwinaanch'uu, Whitehorse gwits'at geedal Ihłoh nigiheedaa gwikwah. Etr'idinii Zheh gijilch'eii. Agadaı kheenjit gugwiłtsaii kwah. Giinleii akoo digidiʔii guuniłʔil Guuzheh gwits'at niizhit, ezhit gwizrih gijilch'eii. Nugwidadhı juutin juutin ts'at tik, gwiintl'oo gwitr'it gwidhaatsaii. Khants'ı Whitehorse gwits'at Bishop Greenwood shidinjii hah giinkhi Neʔtr'oojiłnaii, nandhadii kwah, ts'at dinehtl'eh shintl'atchul James duuyeh khant akoo dindiʔih yahnuh. Nugwidadhat juuti juutin juutin ts'at tik gwitshudhat. Jii denehtl'eh giikh vintl'ayahaachah. Gwid shidinjiiʔ nugooviłʔii gat'iiniidhan kwal Gwits'at chihshiʔ niidhan. June nant Whitehorse gwits'ı chidhiidaʔoh, nugwidadhat nihk'iitik gagaonahtan. Bisho Greenwood yik'oo giinkheh, Christ tr'igiikhii zheh gwizhi Giikhii tr'ałtsaih. Gwiintl'oh sheenjit gwiinzii, shidinjii giikh gwadal nadaazhii geenjit shoh ihłih, jidii tthak nikhah t'iidiʔih. Geetak nakhweenjit gugoontrii. Nakhwo nich'it, nakhwo chaatsı guukwah, aii ts'at nakhweenjit gwiizuu. GaninjiʔihdhI to tell me. When he handed me the letter I said, "No James. Don't be in a big hurry. Big hurry, 33 years? Let's take the letter to the Minister."

It was a hard decision, but my husband wouldn't rest. He just wanted to go. We went to Whitehorse in June and again he went into training for six months. Then he was ordained by Bishop Greenwood in Christ Church Cathedral.

It was a relief and the biggest thing that happened in my life. I was so happy to see my husband in clerical clothes. We did everything together. Sometimes we had a hard time. We lost our dear daughter and our dear little son. We took it hard. I don't want to remember that. Sometimes he felt downhearted about what was going on but he always had a smile for his people. He joined them in a joke, in dancing and in service with prayers.

People nowadays never go by without mentioning him to me whenever they see me.

— *Sarah Simon*

IN 1928 the flu killed my dad. He had been a minister for a long time. There were only two of us in the family, my brother Lazarus and me. The people wanted one of us to become a minister. Lazarus was older and had never been able to go to school so it would have been very hard for him. I was still young then and I'd been to school in Hay River. I told him I would think about it.

I made up my mind I would do it. There was nowhere for me to get more schooling so I left Fort McPherson and went to Aklavik where I worked for the mission. They had their own hospital there. At the same time the ministers taught me. That was in 1929. I met my wife there. We both worked for the mission. I was ordained a minister in 1943 and I served for 30 years.

— *Jim Sittichinli*

gat'iinihdhan kwah. Aii guugaa dinjii tat ts'at shoh nil: Tr'igiinkhii gwizhit guuvah t'iinch'uh, atr'adzoo guuvah nehe Juk drin tth'eii giiyeenjit giinkhii, nijin shiganahʔii daiʔ. Sara Simon.

1928 gwinoo ƚlu hah shitiʔ vakwah. Nugwidadhat gwiinle gwizhit giikhii iinliʔ. Neekant zrih iidaalii. shoondee Lazar hah. Ihƚee giikhii viliʔ nakhwoo guunuh. Lazarus vaghaiiʔ lei shiiʔaii school gwits'at chidhiizhii kwah, ts'at shiiʔaii shighai leii kwaa aii tl'ee gwinoo Hay River School gwits'at chidhiizhi GaninjiʔhihdhAt vaƚnuh. Akoo dahiishaʔaa nihdhan. Ihƚak h school nihihshaa gooʔaii kwah. Aii ts'at Teetl'it Zhe gehƚichiidhiizhii, Aklavik gwits'at chidhiizhii. Giikhii ka eenj gwitr'it t'igwiƚʔih. Eƚts'ik zheh chan gwidiʔin. Ezhit da shitr'iinjoo uudhiinjik, nikhah tr'igiikhii geenjit gwitr' t'ugwaaʔih. 1943 giikhii shitr'iƚtsaih. Nugwidadhat juutin juuti juutin gwitr'it t'ugwaƚʔih. Jim Sittichinli.

Ihƚat gwinoo, oonjit dinjii neekaii shitiʔ eghee zhe gwadhoh niniintthaii. Shitiʔ giikhii iinliʔ. Drin zhit tr'igiikh tr'igwahtsii. Dinjii zhuh kat eenjit. Aii oonjit neekaii tr'igiikh nanugidaʔoh. Iitsii vah itr'idlii, iitsii uuzhuh, shitiʔ edlih dan

Jim Sittichinli
Photo: Dept of Information GNWT.

ONE time two white men put their tent right beside my father's. My dad was a minister and he held a service every Sunday for the Loucheux People. These white men came into the Sunday Service. One had a guitar and the other a trumpet. When my father started to sing a hymn they played. By Gosh! It sounded pretty good to me. I'd never heard anything like that before.

— *Andrew Kunnizzi*

IN those early days there was no school. The mission taught the children but most of the boys never came to school. They were out in the bush learning how to hunt.

— *Jim Sittichinli*

ezhit giiyitdahɬih, gwiintl'oh sheenjit gwiinzii. Gwitshih gwijihdh'ak kwah. Andrew Kunnizzi.

Yeʔeenoo daiʔ, gaonahtan zheh kwah. Giikhii kat tr'iinin gagoonaɬtan, chaa kat giinleii kwah ts'at ezhit gugwinahʔih kwah. Nihk'yuu gwitat gwaʔan nugaazrii. Jim Sittichinli.

Fort Providence dant RC gaonahtan zheh gooʔaih. Tsiigehtshik gwits'at dinjii zhuh tr'iinin kat gwits'ee nugadadal. Hay River dant chan geʔtr'oonahtan zheh ezhit dinjii zhuh tr'iinin kat gwits'ee nugadadal. Nugwidadhat nihk'iidaang nakhwohant nakhwotiʔ guunaaʔih kwah. Igidint'eh nakhwoganahʔih kwah. Jidii iidaaʔaa nakhweenjit nizii, jidii nakhwa gatr'oonaatan gwiintsal, guugaʔ gwits'at gugwaaʔaih. Sarah Simon.

Shahant shitshih daiʔ, school iindiʔ gatr'uunuhtin, shuunuʔ. School gwits'at chihshih gat'iinihdhan kwah. Diiyeejii kat diits'at k'agwigwahdhat, guugaa gwits'at chidhiizhii. Drin tik gwizrih niginjik zhit giniikhih, aii tl'ee at'at duuyeh akoo digwinuu diigahtsih. Aii ginjik zhit tr'igiinkhih kwah. Ezhit daiʔ French zrih goonlii. Nugwidadhat ihɬak gik'iniljik, guuk'yuu ginihkhii. Gehndoo nugwidadhat gashitr'oonaɬtin gwiintsal. Ezhit daiʔ gwanoo shitiʔ vigwidiinjik ts'at vakwah. Sheenjit

At Fort Providence there is a convent school where lots of Red River Indians went. The Loucheux children went to Hay River Residential School. In the old days when we went to school we never saw our parents for seven or nine years.

We never went home and no one from home visited us. We didn't eat well but what we had was good for us and what little education we got from there, we used it!

— *Sarah Simon*

My mother was in school before me and wanted me to learn. I didn't want to go to school. The grey nuns picked on you and treated you like a child. But I went. You spoke your language for only three days and after that they cut you off. You couldn't speak your language anymore.

At that time there was only French. In one year's time I learnt to talk and understand them. The next year I started my schooling and I learnt a little. That same year my dad died in an accident. I was really sad and didn't know what to do. The second year my grandfather adopted me and he sent for me. The English School had just started then.

When I was fifteen years old I worked for white people. I started learning a-b-c-d, and I used to make up words out of that. That's how I taught myself to read.

—*John Blondin*

gwiizuu, dahiisha?aa gahshindaih kwah. Gehndoo nugwidadhat shitsii shuunkagiinkhih, vah t'ihihch'aa eenjit. Jukwaahee oonjit k'yuu gagootr'oonaatan. Shighaii? ihłogwidjuutin ts'at ihłogwinli? ihłih, ezhit dant oonjit kat eenjit gwitr'it t'igwił?ih. Aii tł'ee ABCD aii ak'ilnjik. Aii tł'ee gwik'it tegihikhyaa akoo ts'ants'at geedoodinidhiłtin. John Blondin.

Mary Wilson ganadhandaih. Aklavik dant ge?tr'onahtan zheh iindi?. 1928, 1933 gwinoo.

Ganałdaih. Tr'ih choo nitshii gwizhit, zhit gwits'at chiidhiizhii. Gwiinzii ganałdaih kwah. Shijuu vaghaii? tik gwilih, aii tł'ee vaghaii? leii shahchuuzhii. Aklavik dant RC ge?tr'oonahtan zheh dant k'aiididal, tr'iinin ka leii hah. Tik juutin akoo nich'it dinaanch'uu. Aii gaa sheenjit gwiinleii. Shiti?, Shahant hah shik nihk'yuu hee tthan? gugwich'in. Tr'iinin goonlii gwinah?ii kwah. Ge?tr'oonahtan zheh nik'ehduk zheh goonlih. Gwitshih dai?, akoo diinch'ii zheh gwinił?ih kwah. Zheh gwiintshii k'it shah t'ugoonch'uh. Tr'oochit nugwidadhat tr'iiniizhii diidhahkhaii. Tr'oochit oonjit jiitth'ak kwah. Tthak ts'at diiginjik zhit tr'igiinkhih kwah. Diiyeenjit tsingwidjahnch'uu. Ganałdaih. Tł'aa iival kat dadhiidii, niizhit

Mary Wilson.
Photo: Dept of Information GNWT.

Mary Wilson remembers her school days spent in the residential school at Aklavik from 1928 to 1933.

I REMEMBER when I went to school on the steamboat called *SS Distributor.* That's when everything started for me. I hardly remember before that. My sister was three or four years older and she came with me.

We arrived in the convent in Aklavik with all kinds of kids. There were about thirty girls. It was such a big crowd to me. My parents lived in the bush, you never had so many kids in one place.

The mission was only a two-story building but I'd never seen a house before. It looked like a twenty-story tower to me! I was very, very lonely, especially in the first few months when I couldn't understand a word of English. Nobody spoke their own language at all. Everything was

gwits'at ejihtth'ak. łaii jihtth'ak. khaiinjii ihtreh. shighaiiʔ nihk'iitik gwidilii.

Ezhit gwahniaʔyiaa gwitshih French k'yuu tr'igiinkhih. aii tl'ee chan oonjit k'yuu. Shitshih daiʔ geʔtr'oonahtan zheh gwits'at chuujil. Fort Providence aii ts'at Fort Resolution dant. French aguutr'oonałtan. Gwiintsal French jihtth'ak. diiyeejii guuk'iigheʔ. Tr'oochit nugwidadhat zhit ginjik eenakhwoogoonałtan. Ejiidahłii chan juuts'ants'at "Nakhwo chiigheʔ ohzruk. nakhwo ninʔ k'eeʔohtrah". Nugwidadhat gwahgwan guuzhik at'at duulee oonjit k'yuu ginihkhih. Drin tsal tshih srii tik ahshuk ezhit t'ihch'uh. Diiyeejii dinehtl'eh nakhwats'an ałtsaii. nakhworiʔ vakak dhaʔaih. jidii nohthan. vakak nigoonohłih. Santa Clause eenjit. Nitr'ijilzhii dant nugoodhiłʔih.

Gwid dugwidiʔih gahshindaih kwah. Gwiintsal ts'at gwizrih oonjit k'yuu ginihkhih. Akoo diinihdhan. ch'ik nihdhan. jidii niidhan shahnuh. Ch'ik jihnuu. shits'an tr'iłtsaii jiʔ. ganałdaih kwah.

Ezhit tsiitr'eediʔiʔ. Gwiintl'oh geenjit ninjiʔihdhat. Elig nizii etr'idiih. gwiintl'oh shah gwiinzih. ganałdaih. Vant

so strange; the people, the language, the place. I remember sitting on the swing and I heard a dog howl in the distance. I cried I felt so sad. I was six years old.

Just before we got there, they had changed the language of instruction from French to English. The ones who went to school before me to Fort Providence and Fort Resolution had all been taught in French. I did learn a little bit of French from being around the nuns and brothers and fathers. They all talked among themselves in French.

The first year they started to help us learn the language. We sang action songs like, This is the way you wash your face, brush your hair.

Before the year was out, I was able to speak some English. Just before Christmas I must have been there for about three months by then, the nun who supervised us, got us all together. She had a paper with everybody's name on it and she was asking us what we wanted from Santa Claus. I was waiting in line but I didn't know what was happening. I was picking up a little bit of English but I didn't know what to say to her. The word dishes stuck in my mind, I don't know why so when she asked me what I wanted I just said dishes! I don't remember if I got any.

They had a concert that fall. That really impressed me. They sang *Rock of Ages* and had something set up with smoke going up. It was like something out of this world. That and the singing really struck me. I can remember now the way I saw it through a child's eyes.

We went to school all morning until lunch time then from 1:00 pm to 3:30 pm. We didn't have recess. We learnt reading, writing, and arithmetic, how to multiply and subtract, nothing like algebra. Sometimes now I wonder how far I would have gone if I had had the chance. When gwitugwinaanch'uu geʔtr'oonahtan zheh gwits'at tr'eedah, aii tl'ee chan uuʔan neetr'adal. Ezhit dant ganakhwatr'oonałtan, ediniiditl'oh, edinehtl'eh kak tr'igiinkhii. Juk geetak ganinjiʔihdhat. Gwindoo gashatr'oonahtan jiʔ nihdhan. Gashuunaatan shigwitr'it tthak gwiizih. Salak kat shagat'iiniidhan kwah, aii koo diinihdhan gwiizii shigwitr'it t'igwiłʔih kwaa jiʔ, duuyeh dishagahdhan nihdhan. Diiyeejii kat t'ehshit gwiiyeendoo ch'anuh ts'at diigijaaʔeh. Jidii ejuk ts'at gwitr'it t'agwaaʔii gwiizuu nakhwotr'ahnuh. Gwiizih kwaa gwits'at tiinhaa nakhwagahnuh.

Gwid gwiizii gwitr'it t'ugwaaʔih jiʔ, zheekat gwits'at khohdaa ginuh. Juk uunjiʔ nugwinałʔik, gwiizii dinjii ts'at t'iginuh kwaa' Aii tl'ee tsheeniidadal, tsiiʔiidiʔih, dachaavał hah gwideechaajak. Aklavik han gwinjik gooʔaii. Tthan tsiiʔiidiʔih. Ezhit geʔtr'oonahtan zheh gwidii tthał naadhiʔeh.

we had exams I always got top marks. I never had trouble with my schoolwork.

A lot of my friends didn't like me because of that and I felt rejected. I used to wonder if I should make mistakes on purpose so I could be at their level and so they wouldn't hold it against me.

The nuns pushed religion too much. Everything we were taught was if you did something it was a sin. If you did it you'd go to hell. If you didn't do it you were going to Heaven. Everything was sin, sin. Some of the missionaries now, when they look back, they realize they did harm to the people. It made some people very confused.

After they let us out of school we played outside with sleds, and toboggans. Aklavik is on the Peel River and we used to slide down the riverbank. We made our own fun. There was a fence around the mission and we weren't allowed to go beyond it.

The boys and girls were not allowed to play together. We had chores. The little ones used to sweep the snow off the steps. The older ones looked after the dining area and made sure it was clean. They washed the floor every weekend.

We learned cooking by helping out in the kitchen. One of our supervisors was a nun who was a seamstress. She made all the clothes. As soon as we were older she taught us how to sew on an old treadle machine. That came in handy for me later on.

We had to wear black outfits with trimmings for our school outfit. For Sunday, for going to church, we had another one and for big feast days we had another. It had a white veil. The boys wore suits. The pants came way up to the knee with long stockings. I remember after I was married we would visit around and talk about our

Nich'it, chyaa ka hah nikhah tsiigidiʔih, gwitr'it gwitsal gidiʔih. Tr'iinin tsal kat gwineetee zhoh gehłeegilih. Tr'iinin vighaiiʔ leii, atr'aʔaa zheh gwizhit gwik'eegahtrah, drin yeet'ii dant. Vik'eʔtr'ahch'uu diiyah gahgoogwitr'aaʔii. Diiyeejii ihłee nakhwok'anahtii. Nakhwo gwich'aa tthak k'ajaakaiʔ ganakhwonahtan vizhit k'etr'ijahkaiiʔ zhit. Aii tl'ee gwinoo vah gwitr'it t'igwiłʔii gahshindaii. Geʔtr'oonahtan zheh edhitl'ii zraii ik geenjit iidaʔih. Drin zhit tr'igiikhii geenjit ezhii gwich'aa iidaʔih. Chyaa kat dhał nizii eeyiduk ik nagadaazhii. Stocking njuh chan zhigijilʔuh. Shitr'uunjik tl'ee geenjit nikhah gwiidinduk. Nits'oo nigwidjaazhiii geenjit iidadlah, chyaa kat stocking njuh zhigijiłʔuh, aii eenjit chan iidadlah.

Diiyeejii gwiintl'oo diits'at k'agwigwahdhat. Geetak laa chigidinjii, tr'iinin k'aganaatii dant, nakhwok'it t'igiinch'uu kwaa goovoojihnuh. Aii tl'ee gwinoo, shighaiiʔ ihłogwijuutin ts'at ihłak gwilii. Shin hee. geʔtr'oonahtan kwah, gwaʔan natshiidadał kwah, chiitaii tl'aaval k'it gwikak dadhiidih. Aii gwits'at chitr'iinʔoo zheh gwits'at tihshaa nihdhan. Ezhit zheh gwiintshii gooʔaii, aii gwits'at ejihtth'ak, gweʔee natshidhilgik. Diiyeejii gwits'at cheedhizhih, akoo diheedaʔaa uujihnuh kwah. Ezhit nakhwok'it t'igiinch'uu kwaa goojihnuh.

Diiyuundee kat gwiintl'oo gwitr'it t'igahʔih. Troo leii gichah, khaii geenjit. Khaii tthak aii geenjit gwitr'it t'igahʔih. Łuu chuujik tl'ee, tr'ih school days. We used to laugh and kid one another about the way we used to dress at school especially the boys' stockings.

The nuns were very strict. Very. Maybe they were impatient sometimes or maybe they were tired being around kids all the time. Because of the way they dressed I never thought they were like us. I thought they were altogether different until I was eleven years old.

There was no school in the summer but we didn't go home. I was sitting outside on the swing when I needed to go to the washroom. The outhouse was a good-sized building and was partitioned off at the back. I heard someone in that part. Kids are curious so I ran back to the swing and I waited. I saw one of the nuns coming out of there. They do those things too! I was so surprised. I didn't think they were human beings.

The brothers who worked there had a lot to do. In the fall time they cut the wood, piled it up and then moved to another spot, cut and piled it again. They did that all winter for the furnace. When the ice moved, the barge came in with cords and cords of wood. It used to be tied down below the mission so we would make a beeline and pass wood one to another. All day we worked like that but we didn't think of it as work. We had fun.

At the same time as they cut wood, the brothers would be fishing. They put up stakes and saved the fish for the winter for us. We ate fish and meat. Aklavik is close to the mountains and some men used to go hunting for the mission.

They got caribou and other meat for us. I was used to that as I was brought up on wild meat. They got their vegetables from Fort Good Hope. The mission there had a great big garden for potatoes, cabbage, carrots and choo zhit, troo leii tr'uunjik, zheh gehchit taatr'ijuhłih. Drin tthak gwitr'it t'igwaaʔii gaa nakhwah gwiizii. Diiyuundee kat łuk kagidiʔii, khaii geenjit. Łuk, nilii hah iidaʔaa, Aklavik ddhah eghee gooʔaii. Dinjii kat vadzaih eenjit nagaazrii. Geʔtr'oonahtan Zheh nilii gwits'an gahtsih. Nilii kan diik'ihdhat. Fort Good Hope gwanshih deek'it gooʔaii, ezhit giikhii t'iinch'uu dant nantgwanahshii, geʔtr'oonahtan gwits'at neegaazhik. Aklavik gwiniik'oo, tr'igwinahshii kwah. Geetak iidaʔah, gat'iinihdhan kwaa googaa iidaʔah.

Diiyeejii, Diiyuundee, nich'it, chyaa ka hah gwizhit tr'aʔaa goonlii. Gehghee tsiitr'idiʔii zheh goonlii. Nich'it kat deek'it kak giłchuh, chyaa kat aii dachanchyah kat. Ełts'ik Zheh gwiintshih kwaa ezhit gooʔaii.

Nugwidadhat ihłogwinliʔ gahshuk shizheh gwinałʔih kwah. Shiginjik anadhiłdeh. Neekat shitiʔ sheenidhiizhii, Aklavik dant , gwat shihant niinzhuk nałʔinʔ kwah, vanadhiłdeh. Nihkhan shitiʔ guuniłʔii kwaa, gehndoo shin jukwaahee gwiintsal shiginjik zhit ginihkhih. Aii gwiirih łoo kwah, nits'oo edigwidaandaii ganałdaih kwah. Geetak gwijaadhak'anʔ dant iidaʔaa gwaatsih gwarih. Ganałdaii, gwitat t'iidach'uh daiʔ, troo iidaachaa, zheh gwadhoh ts'at nahjaazhik. Shoondee vetr'iinjoo niłʔii, vik'it t'ivihch'uʔ nihdhan, nits'oo gwitr'it t'igwahʔii gahdindaii, troo nahjihtik, shuʔ gwiizii turnips. In the fall they harvested and distributed to the missions. Aklavik was too cold to grow anything. But I'll never eat pea or barley soup up until today! I remember how we had to eat it whether we liked it or not. That was the meal!

On the first floor of the mission was the kitchen, the fathers' dining area, the sisters' and the girls' dining area, the boys' dining area and the boys' recreation part. The second floor was our recreation area and the attic where the girls' dormitory was. We were lucky we had beds but the boys slept on the floor. There was a small building at the back that was used as a hospital.

After five years, I went home. I had lost my language. My dad had been to see me twice in Aklavik but I had never seen my mother since I had left. I'd forgotten her. I couldn't remember what she looked like. I couldn't communicate with my parents and they couldn't talk to me.

By the next summer I had begun to talk a little bit but that first year was very hard. I tried to talk, I guess I sounded funny and they used to laugh. Not only that, I'd got used to the way of life in the convent. We used to go out in the woods on a picnic but that was all. I had to learn all about living out on the land again; how to work, how to cut wood, how to pack it on your shoulder and bring it back to where the tents were. I always looked up to my brother's wife. She was so efficient in everything. I always wanted to be like her. I never realized she was so used to doing it, it came easy to her. The way she could carry wood! I tried to carry two sticks, one would go up, one down. Oh the frustration!

We used to move about so much. We moved here and there looking for game or if a place got trapped t'ishi?ii, shik nachiidinjik.

Shik uundaazhih, deek'it guukagwinaa?ih, khyah chan tr'oodlih, khaii hee aih zhitr'ijil?uh. Shoondee, aih nizii sheenjit ałtsaii, gwiintl'oh vat'iinihdhan. Aii zhit natshihdik .gugwił?eh. Chan ge?tr'oonahtan zheh neeshishih k'it t'iinch'uh. Shijuu ihłee gwidilih, shits'at tr'iinjih, aachin k'yuu shits'at giinkhih. Vah gwitat gwa?an gyah dhihtl'ih.

Vits'at gwiintl'oh gik'iilnjik. Gashoonałtin gwik'iighe? gwitr'it gishi?ih. Shidinjii vakwaa tl'ee ndoo ts'at gwitr'it t'igwił?ih.

out we had to move to another location. In the wintertime you have to use snowshoes, the snow is so deep. My brother made me a beautiful pair. I was so proud of them and wanted to try them out.

What a time I had. I used to fall all over the place, buried in the snow. I was in the snow more than on my feet. I had to learn everything over again. Everything was so strange, just like when I first went to school.

I was lucky I had my younger sister who was two years younger than me. She was a great help. We were always together and she spoke Slavey to me all the time. We used to go in the woods and set snares. I used to follow her around.

I don't think school was a waste of time for me. If it wasn't for school, I wouldn't have had a job. I wouldn't be reliable. Even just the little education I had carried me a long way after my husband died.

— *Mary Wilson*

SIDEBAR: ABOUT THE "OIL DISCOVERY"

ACCORDING to the official records, an oil sample was brought to Athabasca Landing from Fort Norman in 1912. In 1914 T.O. Bosworth, a geologist, staked claims to seepages found by local families. In 1920 Imperial Oil bought Bosworth's claims and drilled for oil.

No mention has ever been made in the history books of John Blondin's and of Elizabeth Yakeleya's father who discovered the oil on their land.

– Sarah Stewart

6. Oil Discovery

Khaii Atr'agwahnʔaih.

Dinjii zhuh kat gwits'at gidiʔih kwaa, łiʔ dugwidlii goonlih. Joe Blondin.

"The Natives found it and never got anything and that's the truth."

— Joe Blondin

Fort Norman Oil Company, 30 miles below Fort Norman (Tulita).
Photo: Frame from the film We Remember.

Shitiʔ, Norman Wells dant khaii agwahʔaih. Zheh nihk'iitik ts'at ihłak Guate Van dant t'iidaach'uh. Shreendit, shin hah t'iidaach'uh. Shitiʔ dats'an eenjit nidhizrii, ezhit dant nan zhit gwits'at iizhoo ihłak gwinahʔii. Chuu tat dinaadlat niłʔii. Gwaʔan nadizhii, akoo duguugahnuh, khaii tyah zhah hah gwits'ii hidah. Aii zhit khaii uunjik, zheh gwits'at gichuujil, Hudson Bay dinjii ts'an giiyiłtsaih. Duuyeh aii khaii ihłoh t'iłʔii, goovahnuh, gwid duulee yeenjiʔ neenihʔaih, aii jiʔ nakhweenjit gwiteezaa. Shitiʔ srii ihłak tl'ee vakwah. Ihłat nagwijiitth'ak kwah. 1920 gwinoo oonjit kat k'adadal gwinaaʔih. Dakhwoʔih, jiidanuh. Nan zhit khaii gwidjidhaach'aii

Fort Norman Oil Company Well south of Imperial Oil well at Norman Wells, 1921.
Photo: National Photography Collection Public Archives.

MY FATHER found the oil in Norman Wells. We had seven cabins on Gaute Lake and we used to stay there in the springtime, sometimes all summer. Dad was duck hunting around the shore when he found something strange coming out of the ground. It was boiling like water.

He came home and told the family, "I'll take an empty 2-lb lard pail, put it in there and bring it back." They took the pail with them when they went to town and gave it to the Hudson Bay Manager. He said, "That's oil. I can't do anything with it but I'll ship it out for you. Maybe it'll do you some good."

My dad died about a month after that and we didn't hear anything more. In 1920 we saw white men coming along here.

"What are you doing?"

"Staking an oil claim."

We know nothing about it. My grandfather said to me, "That's the oil your dad found." How did the white men know? There had been no white people in the Mackenzie till then. No trappers. Just the trader.

— John Blondin

ginuh. Gahʔiidandaii kwah, shitsii akoo dashahnuh. Aii khaii nitiʔ yigwahʔaii, oonjit kat nits'oo gahgidindaii. Ezhit gwinoo nagwidchoonjik guutr'anahʔih kwah, khyah dhidlii chan kwah, ookat ahtsii zrih. John Blondin.

Shitiʔ, 1912 khaii agwahnʔaih. Tr'ih choo, steamboat, vaazhii zhit Johnny Berens hah gwitr'it t'agwahʔih. Hudson Bay kat Smith, Tuk gwits'at giizhit gwitr'it t'agwahʔih. Aii gwik'iigheʔ oonjit gwitr'it geʔk'aanjik. Juk gwandaih jiʔ, adant khaii agwahnʔaii gah gweheedandaih. Shitiʔ vakwaa gwits'at ihłak gwidjiidatth'ak kwah. 1918 geʔtr'oonahtan zheh t'ihch'uh, diiyeejii Mary shits'at giikhii. Nitsii nitjin t'iinch'uu lee ganinaandaih. Ezhit dant, juk khaii eenjit gwinitr'igwidjiilih, chyaa kat, Providence, Simpson, Resolution gwits'at, łaii dachaavał hah k'ugidadal, nan egugwidjiłcheii. Nakhwozheh tth'eih ezhit goodlih gwizhit geetak t'iidach'uh. Oonjit kat nagwidchoonjik khyah goodlih kat zrit, shuuʔii nizheh ihłeh gwizhit t'ihdach'uu, ginuh. Nugwidadhat ihłak gahnshuk ezhit t'igiinch'uʔ. 1924 ezhit nugwiinaaʔii, nakhwozheh naʔgwidiinjił. Gwiintl'oh sheenjit gwiizuu. Khaii eenjit gwitr'it t'agwahʔii kat duuleh geenjit ihłoh t'igidiʔii goovoojiidinuh. Oonjit kat khaii agwahʔaii ginuh, shuu t'iginuh. Elizabeth Yakelaya.

Elizabeth Yakeleya as a girl at school in Fort Providence.

MY DAD found the oil in 1912. He was a pilot with Johnny Barens on the Steamboat *Distributor,* that the Hudson Bay ran from Smith to Tuk. That is how he knew about white man's ways. If he had lived it would have been recognized that he was the one who discovered the oil. But after it was shipped out he died and we never heard anything more about it.

In 1918 I was at school and Sister Mary spoke to me. "You know where your grandfather was living? That's where they are drilling for oil. Boys from Providence, Simpson, Resolution have come down by dog team to stake claims."

We still had cabins there where we used to live some of the time. When the white trappers who used to go along the Mackenzie River asked my uncle to lend them one of those houses he always did. They would stay there for a year.

In the fall of 1924 when we went to our cabins everything was smashed. Nothing was left. I feel so bad about it. We thought the oil company might do something but they didn't. They say the white man found the oil but it's not true.

—*Elizabeth Yakeleya*

Khaii atr'agwahʔaii tr'egwehdeetth'ak gwitshih, shitsii uunjiʔ chuuzhih. Ezhit dant khaii ghat gwitr'it gwitr'it t'agwahʔih. Shreendit gwinoo nan kat tthak gwits'at dinjii k'adadal, łaii hah. Khah ontshuh, aih hah. Alaska gwits'at niizhit gwits'at aii khaii eenjit gwitr'it t'ugugwahʔih. San Sault Rapids, Ezhit dant 70 mile ee Norman Wells gehndit 55 mile Fort Norman gehnjit. Nan hiidaʔaa giiniidhan, gwik'it goodlit kwah. Imperial dinjii kat tr'oochit gwits'at nan goonjik. Dinjii kat gwiintl'oh gat'igiiniidhan kwah. Yeenjiʔ gwits'at lizhaa dinjii dugweheech'aa gahgidandaih, gwid nakhwont gwitch'in iidalii ts'at gahʔiidindaih kwah. Itsen dinyaach'iʔ gahdindaih gwits'at gwigwahaaʔah gwid, denehtl'eh kat gwidinidhatl'oh diʔih kwah. Ezhit gwanoo gweedha denehtl'eh zhit jidii tthak goodlii gahgwidindaih kwah. Dinjii danuh, łiʔ dadlii tr'oonuh.

Ddhah ts'at nahtr'idhijił, khyah tr'uudlih, k'anaiidadal tl'ee, tshid nilii, iitsii gał choo nahdalak hah nakhwozheh nagwidinaanaii, aii gwideek'it digizheh gugwiłtsaih. Shitsii, shitiʔ hah khaii, zhuu iiʔan guuts'an tr'ahtsih, dahshuk gugwandaii tthak. Shint'eh chan nugwidadhat neekaii gweedhaa zhuu khaii shits'an tr'ahtsii. Juk Norman Wells oonjit kat ezhit t'iinch'uu. Dinjii zhuh kat duuyeh zheh gwadhoh guuvehghee nigichih. Ezhit shigoonlih, guugaaʔ ezhit taii gwinjik gwirih natshihdik sheenjit goonlih.

Oil drilling crew hauling baulks of timber, Bear Island.
Photo: Frame from the film We Remember, Public Archives Canada.

EVEN before the news came back about the sample my grandfather had sent out,the oil rush was on. That spring half of Canada was down there. People came with dog teams, packsacks, snowshoes. Even from as far away as Alaska.

Everybody tried to get a little cut out of this oil strike. It was staked clean below Sans Sault Rapids, seventy miles below Norman Wells and fifty-five miles above Fort Norman. They figured that if they had property, they would have something but it didn't turn out that way. Imperial Oil had leased the property first and the people who had come in were just froze out.

The outsiders, the money men, knew what was going on but the local individual knew nothing. All ehtsée (grandfather) knew was that he'd get something out of it but he had nothing on paper. Well, who knew about documents or regulations or having a title in those days?

Imperial Oil well, Norman Wells.
Photo: Alberta Archives.

Nakhwizheʔ gahchoh k'it t'igidiʔih. Jii tsingwidjahch'uu guunlih. Imperial dinjii denehtl'eh zhit diguuzriʔ niginiinlih. Gwidinidhatl'oh, gwiniłʔii, Mackenzie 1700 gwinoo khaii agwahʔaih. Ezhit gwanoo, Mackenzie khaii eghee gwinahʔih kwah. Gwid Blondins kat tr'oochit khaii agugwahʔaih. Dinjii zhuh tr'oochit khaii giigwahʔaih gwits'at gidiʔii kwaa, jii łiʔ dugwidilih. Joe Blondin.

Everybody trusted everybody else and took a man's word of honour as the truth. We had moved back to the mountains trapping. When we came back the Government had been in there and bulldozed all our houses down the bank and put up their own buildings. Our houses used to be where the transmitter is now.

My grandfather and my dad got free gas as long as they were alive. I got two cards for free gas and oil for two years and then they disqualified me.

Right now, Norman Wells is a white community. The Natives can't even pitch a tent there. I was born and raised there but all I can do is walk the streets.

They are choking us little by little.

Now this is a great joke. Imperial Oil has got a magazine called *Imperial Revue*. I was reading in there how Mackenzie discovered the oil in 1700 and something.

Mackenzie was never around that oil! The Blondins are the ones who discovered the oil. The Natives found it and never got anything and that's the truth.

— Joe Blondin

EDITOR'S SIDEBAR: ABOUT "TREATY 11" CHAPTER

IN THE SUMMER of 1921 Mr. H.A. Conroy was sent by the Canadian Government to bring Treaty 11 to the Indigenous People occupying the territory north of the 60th parallel and along the Mackenzie River to the Arctic Ocean.

The terms of Treaty 11 were decided ahead of time and there was no room for negotiation. The Indigenous People had to agree to "cede, release, surrender and yield up to the Government of Canada for his Majesty the King and his successors forever, all rights, titles, and privileges whatsoever to the land."

The People would still have the right to hunt, fish and trap but subject to Government regulations and not in areas required for settlement, mining, lumbering and trading. An area of one square mile would be set aside for each family of five but even this could be appropriated for public works.

To show His Majesty the King's satisfaction in the 'extinguishment of all their past claims', money would be paid to the people as soon as the document was signed. Initially each person received $12 and every year after that, $35 for each head of a family. The Chief would receive $32 at the signing and $25 thereafter as well as a medal, a flag and a copy of the Treaty. The Headman would receive $22 at the signing, $15 each year after and both Chief and Headman were presented with an annual suit of clothes.

In addition, there would be a once-in-a-lifetime gift of hunting, trapping, and fishing equipment, axes, handsaws, augers, and a grindstone. The Government would also pay teachers' salaries.

Conroy took Treaty 11 to eight communities that summer of 1921. These were Fort Providence, Fort Simpson, Fort Wrigley, Fort Norman, Fort Good Hope, Arctic Red River, Fort McPherson and Fort Rae. Fort Liard signed in 1922 as Conroy had run out of time.

In every community the people signed and 3,000 names were recorded. The Government took possession of 372,000 square miles of land for an initial payment of $23,368 and a projected annual cost of a further $18,000.

Treaty 11 was signed in Fort Norman on July 15th, 1921 by Albert Wright as Chief and Saul Blondin as Headman on behalf of 136 people. Conroy's signature was witnessed by RCMP Constables Johnston and Campbell, RCMP Inspector Bruce and Bishop Breynat. In Fort Norman, Conroy's assurance had been supported by Bishop Breynat. That was enough to persuade the people to sign.

The Roman Catholic Bishop did not accompany the treaty party to the Anglican community of Fort McPherson. There Conroy met with more resistance. The people there were promised that a preserve would be set aside for them if only they would sign. Fearing the alternative would be to lose all they took the little that was offered only to discover later that the Peel River Preserve had never existed.

In Fort McPherson, the Treaty was signed by Chief Julius and Johnny Kyikavichik, (Johnny Kaye) as Headman, on behalf of the 219 Gwich'in. J. Parson, F.H. Bacon, and James Firth witnessed Conroy's signature on July 28, 1921.

The people were not told that by signing the Treaty they had extinguished their title to the land. Although the Hudson's Bay Company had bought, for only a minimal payment, and Canadian Pacific Railway had been granted vast areas of the Northwest Territories, the land claims of the Native people went unrecognized.

Education and medical relief were provided by the churches up until the 1950s with only little financial assistance from the Canadian Government.

Though Conroy had assured them to the contrary, the Peoples' right to hunt, fish and trap without restriction was threatened by the conservation measures of the *Migratory Birds Convention Act* of 1916 and the *Northwest Territories Game Act* of 1917. Closed seasons were declared on moose, caribou, ptarmigan, wild ducks and wild geese as well as some of the animals trapped for fur. Out of season, the people could hunt only if they were starving.

Conroy died in 1922 and only Bishop Breynat remained to plead for justice and remind the Government of the promises that had been made. But as far as the Government was concerned these were never written down so they had no obligation to fulfill them.

– *Sarah Stewart*

7. Treaty 11

Treaty 11. Nakhwonant kak gwizhit gwiidindaih. John Blondin.

"We know that we did not sell our land."

— John Blondin

Treaty Party at Fort McPherson (Teet'lit Zheh).
L to R. Simon Dundzik, John Martin, Ben Kunnizzi, RCMP officer,
Old Robert, Johnny Kaye, Fred Firth, Chief Julius,
Mr. Conroy, Old William Vittreka. Photo: CBC.

S.99. Fort Norman. Ezhit drin tl'at gwanoo, tr'ih choo k'adaluk, dinjii nitshii ihłogwinliʔ k'adadal. Giikhii choo Breynat, guuveenjit Jimmy Sibbeston, łeet'ehdehdeełaa nilih. Oonjit akoo diginuu, lizhaa nakhwots'an haatsaa eenjit k'aiididal. Dinjii kat akoo diguuvaanuh, yehduk khaiiyiidaadah dant tr'igeekhyah. Chiitaii jidhaach'eii gat'iiniidadhan kwaa ginuh. Duuleh hahtshin. Zheh gwadhoh neekaii niidaatthaii, Conroy chan, niinzhuk gweedhaa nuh. Nihkaa dinjii tthak gwee eeheedaa, lizhaa eenjit tr'igiheekhyah, nan eenjit tr'igiheekhyah kwaa nuh. Vanh, zheh gwadhoh ts'at tthak tr'igchuujił. Juudindee dinjii tshid nilih. Aii zrit Saul Blondin, shitsii, dinjii tshid nilih. Conroy akoo dinuh, King gwinoo chiinhaii shahnuh, dinjii lizhaa ts'an hahntsaa eenjit.

Dinjii kat akwaa giiyahnuh. Aii lizhaa, nan t'ih uujiinuh. Duuyeh

Commissioner Conroy makes Treaty at Fort Providence (Zhahti Koe).
Photo: National Photography Collection Public Archives.

Fort Norman

THAT AFTERNOON a boat came around the point and landed on the shore. Four or five big tall guys came up to us. There was a priest with them, Bishop Breynat and an interpreter, Jimmy Sibbeston.

"If you want to talk we should go up on the bank. We can't talk down here."

"We don't want to sit outside. What if it rains?"

So we put up two tents. When we finished it was late so Conroy said, "Tomorrow everybody is to come here and we'll talk about money."

He never said talk about land.

On the second day the people came back in the morning and they put up the walls of the tent so everyone could hear. The white man said, "Who is the Headman?"

That was Saul Blondin, my grandfather. He was the leader of the people.

Then Conroy said, "The King sent me to the North to give the people some money."

;huu lizhaa, king diits'an ahtsih. Nakhwonan duuyeh gwits'an aatsih. ;wizhit adigwijaandaih. Nakhwonan oodhoonjik ji?, yeenji? t'iihiidich'aa (wah. Zhat nakhwon.an kat gwizrih t'ihiidich'ah. Nakhwonan eenjit ;'idjiidinuh kwaa nuh. Vik'iinjizhit kwaa, shitsii akoo dinuh. Nakhweenjit ii dinjii vits'at tr'igiinkhii ji?, nakhwoginjik jiitth'ak kwah. Danuu, dinjii (at gugwidjiitth'ak kwah. Conroy akoo duguugahnuh. Judin nakhweenjit ;wik'it te?giheekhyaa ooghwoondal.?

Albert Wright. " Ge?tr'oonahtan zheh zhit lee iindi?" "aha?" 'nijindee?" "Montreal" "nits'oo ezhit gwits'at chidhiinzhii?" (shuu giikhii ıiidhan). Zhat dant, giikhii vah t'ihch'uh, Montreal gwits'at chuuzhii, ;hint'eh vah chidhiizhii, ezhit ge?tr'oonahtan zheh t'ihch'uh. Oonjit k'yuu ;wiinzii ginihkhih. Akoo dinuh, aii dinjii viiniidhan ji?, oonohjih. Drin tik :l'ee shitsii akoo dinuh. jidii eenjit dee lizhaa nakhwots'an ghohtsah, ihłak ;eenjit, gwitch'in. King nakhwats'at tr'eheendal niidhan. Nits'oo akoo laheedi?yiaa?.

Yeendoo ji?, nahgwitch'in kat, duuleh guuveenjit itjiich'ii ;wehehkwaa, juk googaa geetak guuvah gwiizuh. Geh dhaaghaih kwaa ji? ;hih hiin?aa gweheekwah. Jii lizhaa uudhiinjik ji?, king nits'at tr'iheendal. Tr'a?aa leii nits'an haatsah, juk drin gwits'at nakhwok'ahnatiaa. Łuh, lidii,

The people said, “No, we are sure you want to give us that money for our land. The King won’t give us that money for nothing. We don’t want to give our land away. It’s our life. If you take our land from us we’ve got no place outside. Where are we going to go? Our land is right here and we stay on it.”

“It is not for your land.”

“We don’t believe it!”

My grandfather said, “We have to find someone to translate for us. This man can’t speak our language and the people can’t understand what he is saying.”

So Conroy said, “Who are you going to get?”

“Albert Wright.”

“Did you go to school?” said Conroy to Albert Wright.

“Yes.”

“Where?”

“Montreal.”

“How did you get up there?” (Said in just the way you do when you think someone is lying.)

“I was staying with a minister here, and when he was transferred to Montreal, I went with him and I went to school there. I learnt to speak English very well.”

So Conroy said, “If you want that guy, take him.”

On the third day my grandfather said, “Why do you want to give us that money? It must be for something.”

“The King wants to help you.”

“How’s he going to do that?”

“One of these days your people will be stuck, have nothing. Even now they sometimes have bad luck. What if you can’t even kill a rabbit? You won’t have enough to eat. If you take the money the King will help you, He’ll give you grub, all the grub you want. From this day we’re going to help you. We will give you flour, tea, bacon, a grinding stone, saw, axe, and shovel.”

luguushuu, chiigwik'ih daa?aii nakhwots'an haatsaa. Tth'eii łoo chiigwik'ih gwitr'it t'igwah?ii, naa?ih kwah. Nakhwiindah vah gwitr'it t'ah?ih. Nan kat nigiinii?aih, chuu giizhit t'iinlik, diginli? hah nagiidanahdhał. Tthak ts'at tr'eedlah. T'ehshit nidii, nits'oo de gwitat gwits'at tr'ooheendal?. Vik'etr'igwahdii ts'at 100 ahdih.

Conroy akoo dinuh. Yeendoo gweheedhaa, jii gweedi? nant kak oonjit gweheelah. Dinjii zhuh yeendoo ts'at gugweheelah. Nakhwah tr'igweheedinduk. Ihłoh t'ighozhit ji?, jii edinehtl'eh zhit nighoozri? hee?aii. Haadhoojih ji?, nakhwoonkak tr'agwahnia?yiaa. Gwiyeendoo gaviidandai? niidadhan, oonjit kat k'adadal, nakhwonant kat jii nin dhohghah shro?, gehdeenjah. Duuyeh nuh. Duuyeh dinjii guuts'at katr'agwahdhat. Łuk kagho?ii, khyah tr'oodlii, nitr'aazrii, jii nan nakhwots'an diinch'uu. Aii tl'ee khaiinkoo drin giikhii choo akoo dinuh. Conroy łi? dadlii, shuu giinkhih kwah. Lizhaa nakhwonan eenjit t'iinch'uh kwah. Aii tl'ee dinjii kat łi? dugwidlii giiniidhan, ezhit dai? dinjii tthak gijiinjik. Giikhii choo k'agwaadhat eenjit gwitr'it t'agwah?ii, aii eenjit aha? giiyahnuh. Giikhii choo ezhit t'iinch'uh kwaa ji?, duuyeh treaty tr'uuheendal.

Tr'igwehdineetl'oo gwitshih, dinjii neekaii tshid giinlih. Akoo

John Blondin with his wife and small child.

John Blondin in 1978 during filming of We Remember.

diginuu, Albert Wright, gwiinzii oonjit k'it giinkhih, aii ts'at Saul Blondin chan Albert Wright, akoo diguuvaanuh, nihjaa ohłih. Gwiintl'oh nizii, nits'oo gwitr'it t'agwahʔii, gahdindaih.

Akoo dinuu, nagwidchoonjik han, srii ts'at shih chii, aii gwinaaʔih. Zheh gwadhoh zhit gwits'at, aii tik gwinohʔih. Ihłoh guuts'at t'igwidiʔii jiʔ, akwaa jiʔ, duuyeh ejuk tr'igwahtsih. Treaty eenjit tr'igwidinidhatl'oh, diiyuuzriʔ tr'iniinlih. Dinjii tshid lizhaa 50 guuts'an tr'ełtsaih. Nakhwant ihłogwijuutin ts'at neekaii nakhwots'an tr'ełtsaih. Gehndoo nugwidadhat ihłogwinliʔ zrih nakhwots'an tr'ałtsaih. Juk drin gwits'at. Denehtl'eh kak, treaty 11 gwiniłʔii, akoo diinihdhan, jadee nakhwonan gwits'an dhaatsaih kwah. Mr. Conroy akoo danakhwahnuu, nakhwonan eenjit t'itr'ahʔii kwah. John Blondin.

1921 geʔtr'oonahtan zheh gwits'at k'aniadik. Ezhit daiʔ, tr'oochit treaty goonlii. Dinjii kat akoo diginuu, nakhwonan tr'uuheekat.?. Shuuʔii akoo dinuh. Norman dant geenjit ginjih tr'adaaghoo, guuvah chiidhiizhii. Jidii geenjit lizhaa nakhwats'an gahtsii, akoo nakhwagahnuh. Ezhit gwanoo łuhch'uh tsal googaʔ duuyeh nihts'at uuniidinjih, etr'inʔii goonlii gahʔiidindaih. Conroy, akoo davaadinuh, duuyeh lizhaa vit'ih gwitr'it t'igwaaʔih kwaa, uuniidinjih. Akoo dinuu, nakhwakatr'inahtii nuh.

"We've never seen a grinding stone come alive. How does it work?"

"I'll show you."

They put the grinding stone on the ground and put water in it and started to roll it by hand. Everybody laughed.

"We can't carry that. It's too heavy. How are we going to take it in the bush? It must weigh a hundred pounds!"

Conroy said, "One of these days there'll be a lot of white people in the North. More white than Indians. If you get lost or anything happens to you, your name will be in this book. If you disappear, they'll know where you are and they will look for you."

"But we are sure the King wants the game or the land. When white people come we are very sure you're going to tell us not to kill this animal or that one."

"No," he said. "There will be no law for your people. Nobody's going to stop you going anywhere. You can trap, hunt, fish anywhere you want. The land is yours."

On the last day the Bishop said, "I think Mr. Conroy is right. He doesn't lie. I'm sure he came here to tell you the truth. The money is not for your land."

Then the people started to think a little bit differently. "It's true, true words," they thought. That was the time that the people really prayed and they knew the Bishop worked for God. That is why they said yes. If it hadn't been for the Bishop there would have been no treaty.

Before the Treaty is signed you have to have two Headmen. The people said, "Albert Wright. He can talk good English. And Zaul Blondin."

Albert Wright said, "We have to have witnesses. You have many but we have none." (He was darn good you know. He knew how things were done outside.)

Naghoozriʔ, denehtl'eh zhit nitr'igwiniinlih, yeendoo jiʔ, oonjit gweheelaa, ezhit jiʔ daghohch'aa gaghwookhwandaih kwah. Gwid jii denehtl'eh zhit naghwoozriʔ, aii k'iigheʔ nakhwah gweheedandaih. Lizhaa hah nakhwak'anahtih. Nakhwonan eenjit t'itr'ahʔih kwah. Duuyeh noozriʔ geenjit ihłoh t'igwinuu, tsuk dinaanch'uu dhohkhaii tr'egwehdeechuh kwah. Aii tl'ee gwanoo, game warden iidaʔih. Elizabeth Yakelaya.

Treaty 11, Fort Norman gwizhit tr'oochit tr'igwiniidhintl'oh, July 15, 1921, Albert Wright, dinjii khehkaiʔ giiyaaʔih. Saul Blondin dinjii tshid nilii, 136 akoo dinjii dinaanch'uu. Conroy, gwidinuutl'oo, niveh t'ahʔii, Johnston, Campbell, Inspector Bruce, niveh t'ahʔii, Giikhii choo Breynat.

Fort Norman gwizhit Conroy danuh. Giikhii Choo Breynat yah gwitr'it t'agwahʔih. Dinjii oozriʔ nigiheelaa eenjit. Giikhii Choo treaty gwits'an tr'ahtsii dant, naaʔih kwah. Anglican, Teetl'it Zheh gwizhit Conroy dinjii leii nahʔih. Dinjii akoo duguutr'ahnuh, oozriʔ dinaadhohtl'oh jiʔ gwiizrih, duuyeh nakhwonan tr'uunjih. Aii tl'ee gwanoo, Teetl'it han dant, nan sritr'iinlik kwaa hee giik'anaanjik.

Teetl'it Zheh. 1921 gwiyeeʔan dinjii leii kwah. Teetl'it Zheh gwizhit oonjit k'yuu gwiintl'oh gigiinkhih kwah. Leii kwah kat denehtl'eh kak gigiinkhih ts'at agadantl'oh. *Dinjii khehkaiʔ, Julius duuzriʔ adantl'oo

Albert Wright said, "Our witnesses are Mackenzie River, the Sun and Bear Rock. We can't see them from inside the tent. We have to go out and look."

Everybody came out of the tent.

"You see these three? If anything happens to one of them, you can do what you want. But if nothing happens to them then you can change nothing."

The Treaty was signed.

The Headmen got $50 and all of us got $12. The second year they cut us down to $5 and still today we get $5. When I read Treaty 11, I said to myself, "How come we never talked about giving our land away?"

Mr. Conroy told us in front of witnesses, "It is not for your land."

— *John Blondin*

IN 1921 I had just come back from school. That was the year the treaty men came. The people said, "What are the white people going to do with us? Are they coming to buy our land?"

My uncle said, "They are going to have a meeting in Norman."

They took me with them. They were explaining why they were giving us the money. In those days we could not even take a crumb of bread from each other because we know that's stealing. We said to Conroy, "We can't take your money because we haven't worked for it."

He said, "We're just looking after you. We have to register all your names because later on there will be a lot of white men and you won't know where you'll be. But your name will be in this book so we will know where you'll be. The money will help you. It's not for your land. Nobody will stop your hunting, your trapping. You will live as before. Nobody will stop you. Nobody will count how many marten you're going to catch."

After a few years we got a game warden.

— *Elizabeth Yakeleya*

Joe Blondin and Chief Zaul Blondin.
Photo: National Museums of Canada, Ottawa.

Chief Albert Wright of Fort Norman (Tulita) in 1921 and his wife Harriet Gladue. Photo: CBC gahdindaih kwah. Dinjii kat jidii geenjit treay nilii gahgidindaih kwah. Akoo digiiniidhan, tr'oochit gwits'at giiyuunjik ji?, duuyeh nan gidi?ih. Gwid Mr. Conroy akoo dinuh, aii geenjit łoo kwah nuh. Jii lizhaa nakhwots'an tr'ahtsii, king gwits'at, tsinehdant hah. Nakhwonan eenjit kwah. Nits'oo gwitshih dai? agwidoondaii, gwik'it t'ighohch'ah. Dahshuk Chigwaazraii, han niinlaii, nakhwots'at kheeninde?din?ii. Duuyeh nakhwonan eenjit ihłoh t'inakhwohtr'ahnuh. Vizhit nitr'aazrii, nin katr'idi?ii, gwitshih daghoo?ii, gwik'it tth'aii nan łoo nakhwoohiidakat kwah. Chigwaazraii ddhah tth'aih hee nijin dhaa?aii dant tth'aih dhaa?aih. Han chan niinlaih, gwid tshid nilii kat daginuu, giik'anahtih kwah. Ganaadaih, zhuu nakhwots'at gigiinkhih łeh. Jim Sittichinli. *Dinjii khehkai?, Julius, treaty eenjit oozri? dinuutl'oh.

Dinjii khehkai?, Julius, Conroy oodahkat. Treaty uudhiidinjik ji? lee duuyeh vadzaih eenjit naazrih, duuyeh chan nan kat natshiidinjik?. Duuleh noozrih. Nakhwonan gwichaa, nan kat dant łuk eenjit gwiinzih, vadzaih eenjit natr'aazrii eenjit gwiinzih, aii guugwaa?aih. Ezhit dant zheh gwehee?aa, edinehtl'eh kak gugwijilcheii gwi?ii gwikak ninohłih. Oonjit aii gwidindhitl'oo gwinah?ii ji?, gehłeeheedah. Yeenji? chuu tl'it Gyuu Dizhoonjik, tsiigehtshik gwits'at 100 mile gwidilii. Tsiigehtshik gwitch'in

Fort McPherson

IN 1921 only those very few people who stayed in Fort McPherson spoke English. Few people knew how to read or write. Chief Julius didn't even know how to sign his name. The people didn't understand what the treaty was for. They thought right from the start if they took it, they would lose their land. But Mr. Conroy said,

> "That's not the way it's to be. The money is given to you from the King to make peace, not for your land. You will continue to live the way you did in the past. As long as you see Black Mountain, and see that the River still runs, we make this promise. We won't bother you for your land or any other way of life. You can hunt anytime you want, any animals you want, the same as you did in the past. We are not buying the land."

Black Mountain is still where it was, the River still runs, but the Government never kept their promise. We remember what they told us and we know now they lied to us.

—Jim Sittichinli

CHIEF JULIUS asked Conroy, "If we take the Treaty does it mean that we can't hunt caribou and travel on the land?"

"You can hunt all over, you can have a preserve where there is good fishing and caribou hunting. Put up posts and write Indian Department on them. When any white man around here sees the signs, he will walk away."

The boundary of the preserve went this side of the shore, around the point, along Snake River, all the way up to Arctic Red River, way over a hundred miles.

It was just for the Arctic Red River and Peel River Indians.

The chief said, "There's nothing on that land, not much fur or caribou, some moose but not much. But even so the Government will let us keep it so no white man can go on it."

The next year the Indian Agent said, "The paper about that land is lost." Lost! The Government doesn't believe what the Indians say about the Preserve. But all the people know. It is our land.

—Peter Thompson

kat, teetl'it gwitch'in dinjii zhuh eenjit gwizrih. Dinjii khehkaiʔ akoo dinuh. Gwiyeeʔan aii nan kak nin katr'iheedaʔyiaa goonlih kwah, getak vadzaih, dinjik hah leii kwah. Gwid tshid nilii, aii gwik'anahtii nakhwahnuh. Duuyeh oonjit gwizhit gwinahʔih. Indian Agent akoo dinuh. Aii nan eenjit denehtl'eh zhit gwidindhitl'oo, vah tr'igweedinduk goovahnuh. Dinjii tshid nilii, dinjii zhuh danuu, gwik'iinjizhit kwaa, aii nan eenjit. Gwid dinjii kat nakhwonan t'iinch'uu ginuh. Peter Thompson.

Mr. Conroy, dinjii khehkaiʔ Julius denehtl'eh kak oozriʔ niniinaih ahnuh. Jaghaadee?. Treaty lizhaa nakhwots'an haatsaa. Nah gwitr'it t'agwahʔii kat hah oozriʔ ninohłih. Gwid dinjii khehkaiʔ Julius gwiintsal ninjiʔahdhat. Yeedit ddhah choo Chigwaazraii nohʔii, duuyeh giłaataach'it? Aii gwik'it duuyeh un nakhwotr'anjii. Jii lizhaa oodhoonjik jiʔ. Conroy iitsii vakak dinjii khehkaiʔ tshid nilii, king nihkhah diginliʔ guunjii, vakak dhaʔaih. Jii vakak gwinahʔih. Aii dinjii neekant nihłiʔ goonjii gootr'ichiłʔee. Aii gwik'it tshid nilii nakhwots'at akoo didiʔih. Johnny Kaye. *Johnny Kaye dinjii tshid, Teetl'it Zheh, 1921 gwanoo iinliʔ, treaty 11 eenjit oozriʔ dinuutl'oh.

Dinjii khehkaiʔ Julius, veenjit łeeteedehdihłah, Flyn Harris ts'at giinkhii dant. Indian Agent, Dr. Harvey, Dr. Trustall kahah. Gwiinleii akoo

Indian Treaty Medals were struck without dates and issued at the signing of the seven Indian Treaties between 1871 and 1877. Dates and treaty numbers were stamped as issued.

MR. CONROY told Chief Julius to sign the paper. "What is it for?"

"We're going to give you Treaty money. You and your council have to sign for it."

But Chief Julius was still reluctant.

"You see the great big mountain? Black Mountain? No one will ever move it and no one will ever push you around after you take this money."

Conroy showed him a medal and on it was a governor and a king shaking hands.

"You see this picture? These are two important people shaking hands. Just the same as the Government is doing with you."

—Johnny Kaye

dinuh jihtth'ak. Conroy akoo dashahnuu, oonjit kat duuyeh nakhwonan kat ts'iivii geheechah. *Aii nan dhok nakhwots'an tr'ałtsaih. Tsiigehtshik, Teetl'it Zheh hah gwits'at. Aii googaa yagwinoo ts'iivii leii gwits'at kwaa tr'igwałtsaih, oonjit kat shuu dahkat kwaa goozhik akoo digwidiʔih. *Teetl'it han, nan hah. Sarah Simon.

Juk drin gweedhaa zhit akoo diginuh. Nakhwonan ookat dhohtsaih. Aii geenjit tshid nilii, dinjii kat gahgiheedindaii gugwahtsii kwaa. Aii gwizhit gwitr'it gwiłtsaii. Aii nan dinjii zhuh ts'an tr'ałtsaih, khaii eenjit gwitr'it t'agwahtsii eenjit ts'an giiyiłtsaii. Nakhwant ihłat gwits'at giidiʔih kwah. Gwid dinjii tshid nilii akoo danakhwahnuu, tsinehdant hah treaty nakhwots'an tr'ałtsaih. Nan eenjit łoo kwah. Jim Sittichinli.

Oonjit kat nakhwonan guunjii gat'iiniidadhan kwah. Nakhwonan gwits'an aatsii gat'iindadhan kwah. Vizhit gatr'agwahʔaih jiʔ. Nakhwant'eh viiniidadhan. Un nakhwotr'anjii gat'iindadhan kwah. Oonjit gwizhit chiłʔee adadaatsii. Aii tł'ee yeenjiʔ daganant kat gwits'ee gahdadal, ezhit dant chiłʔee giinlih, nakhwant goozhik khaii chan ts'at geh hah kan gwiidindaih. Sarah Simon.

I USED to translate for Chief Julius when he spoke to Flynn Harris, the Indian Agent or to Dr. Harvey or Dr. Trustall. A good many times I have heard him say,

"Conroy told me that no white man would cut down a tree on our land. That land that was set aside for us from Red River to McPherson. Yet how many trees have been cut down there? I don't think any white man has ever come here and asked me first."

—Sarah Simon

NOWADAYS they say, "You have sold your land." That's why the government never consult the people about the work that's done on the land.

They give the Native land away to the oil company, to different mining outfits and we don't get anything out of it. But the Government told us it was a peace treaty. They said it wasn't for the land.

—Jim Sittichinli

WE DON'T want the white man to take over the land. We don't want to let our land go. We want to hang onto it. If anything is found on it we want to be a part of it. We don't want to be just pushed away while the white man gets rich. He goes back to the outside and settles down richly while we live on lard and rabbit.

— Sarah Simon

. Johnny Kaye. Gah?iidindaih. Nakhwonan ookat dhaatsaih kwah. Nagwidadhat gwiinleii nakhwonan gwizhit gwiidindaih. Gwiizii gwiidindaih, gehdant t'iidich'uh kwah. Shik nakhwah gwijiinzrih. Gwaakwaa nakhwots'at tr'igooheendal?. Shanan tr'oonjii gat'iinihdhan kwah. Dinjii kat nan kat gugwandaih, gwiintl'oh gwitr'it t'igugwah?ih. Shik guuvah nan kat uundizhih goonlih. Gwizhit adagwidaandaih, gugoontrii googaa? guuveenjit ihłoh t'igoonch'uh kwah.

I Don't Want My Land To Go

We know that we did not sell our land.
For many years we lived on our land.
We lived well and nothing ran short.
All the time it is plentiful.

Why should it be taken away from us?

I don't want my land to go.
I don't want it taken away.

Our people live on the land.
We work hard.

And still the land is plentiful.
We make a living and we don't realize it is hard.

— Johnny Kaye

SIDEBAR: ABOUT "THE SICKNESS" CHAPTER

When white people came to the North, they brought diseases to which the people had no natural immunity. Outbreaks of tuberculosis, Spanish flu, and measles killed so many that in some places the birth rate was far exceeded by the number of deaths.

But the flu of 1928 was the worst epidemic. As the steamboat SS *Distributor* sailed down the Mackenzie to the Arctic Ocean, she brought the sickness to every community she visited. Six hundred people, one-sixth of the total Indigenous population, died that summer.

Disease afflicted every family and killed indiscriminately, taking even the young and the strong. Most communities had no medical services.

Disease ravaged the North. Deaths from tuberculosis alone were fourteen times the national average. In 1937 the Government cut off funds for all hospital treatment of Indians suffering from tuberculosis or any other chronic conditions. The situation was officially described as hopeless.

– Sarah Stewart

8. The Sickness

Ts'ik Goonlii. Tth'an k'it gwiintshii goonlih, aii ts'at niht'iʔdeʔii leii aatsii. Elizabeth Yakelaya.

"'The graveyard is so large and we have
to make so many crosses."

— *Elizabeth Yakeleya*

Dene children in hospital in Fort Norman (Tulita), 1945.
Photo: Indian and Northern Affairs Public Archives.

The sickness was officially described as hopeless.
Photo: Frame from Film We Remember.

IN THOSE DAYS we didn't know about TB. We didn't know what it meant. I had twelve children but I only had two boys. The eldest learnt how to work but the second one always followed me. So I taught him how to snare and set fish nets.

He had been playing outside and when it was time for him to come in, he started bleeding from his nose. We took him to the hospital and the doctor said he was having a haemorrhage. He didn't want to stay there and he cried but we had to leave him.

In the fall he said, "Mom, I want to go home with you."

The doctor said, "I'm sorry. I thought he was going to get better but I don't think he will live."

I told him, "Even though he has TB, I will take my son and he can stay with me until his end."

So we took him back. It was in March that he passed away. It was a beautiful morning and the sun was shining. He said, "Please take me to the window. I'll see the sun rising."

I kissed him and I had my tears.

"Mom, please don't cry."

That's the last words he gave me.

I had twelve children, eight of them died.

When the doctor came into the community, he examined many people and said they had TB. He sent many children away to hospital and it was a long, long time before they came back again.

When our children pass away it is a great sadness. Our Dear Lord helps us.

—Elizabeth Yakeleya

In 1928, after the steamboat left, we weren't expecting sickness. An old man had it first but we didn't realize that the flu had started. That year we Willow Lakers came with about twenty tents and there were many people from Bear Lake too. It hit us just as we were getting ready to leave so we couldn't go. Every day people died.

— *Elizabeth Yakeleya*

AFTER the boat arrived here people started to get sick and then they started dying. Myself, Peter Alexie, and another guy went by schooner down to Aklavik because they had a doctor there. But when we arrived, they gave us a policeman instead of a doctor. By gosh! I don't like that. We want a doctor. People are dying. (I didn't say that. I just thought it.) I was sure it was a big mistake. The doctor told the policeman how to treat the people and wrote it down for him. When we came back here the police helped us. The churches were full of patients.

Some boys went down Black Mountain and shot one caribou and brought it back and made some soup. Well of course the people can't sit and eat it. Everyone is too sick, and as for us we should be eating but we're too busy digging graves.

—*Andrew Kunnizzi*

IT WAS in the summer of 1928 when the flu came in by Steamboat *Distributor*. It was almost a week after the boat left that the people started to get sick. I think about 50 people died in Fort McPherson within a week. There was no doctor.

Towards the end, people were dying too fast and only a few people were able to dig graves. It was during July and they had to bury them right away. You can't leave them out.

We used to dig a grave for six people and we had to bury them without a coffin. We put two coffins, one at each end, and put the ones with no coffins in the middle and put lumber over them. We buried them that way.

—*Jim Sittichinli*

Top. SS Distributor moored at Fort Norman (Tulita), and
Bottom. SS Distributor moored Fort Good Hope (K'asho Got'ine), 1929.
This steamboat brought the flu epidemic
to every port along the Mackenzie River.

Photo: University of Alberta Archives, Louis Romanet Collection.

"Indian Graveyard," Aklavik.
Photo: Frame from Film We Remember. Public Archives Canada.

In Fort Norman there was no doctor, no nurse and nobody knew what was happening. The flu didn't last long, not even two weeks, but it wiped us out. We have to bury the dead but still we are always two or three behind. The graveyard is so large and we have to make so many crosses.

Some people came here from Franklin to trade at the Hudson Bay here. On their way back home some of them died too. My cousin needed me so I went to her. I knew she was dying. She said, "Sister, please pray for me and God will help me."

I didn't have tears I felt so bad, no tears.

Before I went back home, they sent word that my uncle had died. I also got a touch of it and Grandpa looked after me. When we have the sickness, we become delirious. I didn't even know where my children were. When I got better, they told me how many people died.

It was thirty people.

—*Elizabeth Yakeleya*

SIDEBAR: ABOUT "URANIUM" CHAPTER

THE MINE at Port Radium was opened in 1932 on Great Bear Lake. Gilbert LaBine is said to have discovered it and he certainly staked the claim. Gold was discovered in 1933 in Yellowknife. The mineral wealth of the Northwest Territories attracted so many outsiders that their numbers grew from a little over a hundred in 1901 to almost 4,000 in 1941.

– Sarah Stewart

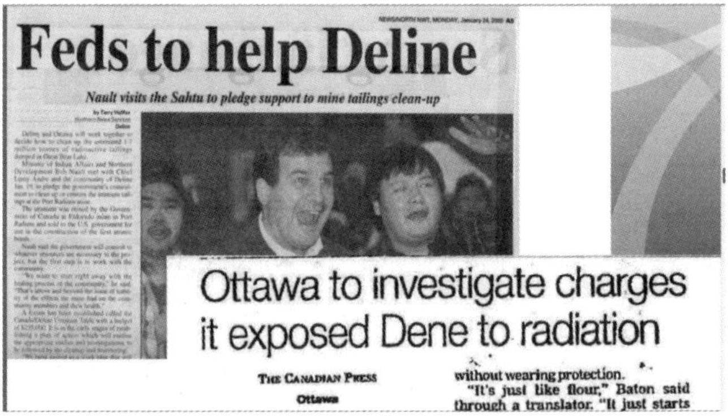

Montage of headlines about Deline, exposure to radiation and the sorrows of the "Village of Widows."

Source: Aboriginal Affairs and Northern Development Canada website.

9. Uranium

Chii litsii. Atr'agwahʔaii daiʔ, neekat gwijuutin zrih iinlih.

— Joe Blondin

"All it amounted to was twenty dollars to the Natives for the discovery."

— *Joe Blondin*

First load of uranium concentrate flown from Great Bear Like to Fort McMurray.
Photo: National Photography Collection.

Sign on display at Port Radium.
Photo: Frame from Film We Remember, 1978.

Sacks of uranium concentrate awaiting shipment at Port Radium, 1939.
Photo: Frame from Film We Remember, 1978.

GILBERT LABINE and Jack St. Paul made a strike over in Hunter Bay. They flew Gilbert LaBine back the next year, to get some more samples. There was a little but not enough so he had to look.

He had to go south to the edge of the lake where he had a spot where the plane was supposed to pick him up. On the way he met Old Beyonnie. His son-in-law is Victor Beyonnie who was the Chief of Franklin for a number of years until he had his accident.

Beyonnie told us that he had a camp at Echo Bay right at the actual mine shaft. As LaBine was the prospector Beyonnie gave him a rock which happened to be silver with pitch blend attached.

LaBine got all excited and gave Beyonnie $20 and a promise that he would get a certain percentage. There was nothing on paper, he had no legal rights. All it amounted to was $20 for the discovery. This is history. Those Old Timers, they don't lie.

I used to be a pilot with the Northern Transportation Company Limited.

They had only one boat on the Mackenzie at the first. Then they bought the Hudson Bay outfit of two or three boats. That's how the machinery came into Bear Lake.

In those days you had to move twelve to fourteen tons with block, jack and tackle pulleys. In 1933 or 1934 the first uranium came across Bear Lake down Bear River through the Mackenzie and out to Port Arthur.

Nothing was said to us about it. We thought it was something like gold. We didn't know the difference anyway. The LaBine Brothers made millions until the Government took over in 1939 when the war started. It was the richest uranium mine in the world at that time. That's Echo Bay Mine on Great Bear Lake.

Discovered by an Indian.

—Joe Blondin

PEOPLE lived all around Bear Lake. I knew Old Beyonnie. He lived about 180 miles east of Bear Lake and he had pitched his tent right on top of the uranium. He didn't know what it was.

He thought it was something like gold or iron and he wanted to show Gilbert LaBine where it was. "Look there's some fancy coloured rock down there!"

They opened the mine in 1931-32 and quite a lot of people came in from all directions, prospectors and businessmen. The place where they found the uranium was called LaBine Point and they had another town next to it called Cameron Bay. They had liquor and sold beer.

The first job I got was in 1939 when I was nineteen. I worked on the boat with the Northern Transportation Company Limited hauling the uranium out. We had to do it the hard way without forklift trucks. They shipped out barge loads of it.

The Hudson Bay on Bear River and other people with scows hauled freight. NTCL only had a fifty-foot open rapid boat then. The Hudson Bay brought up two big boats. But still they had to build a bigger one. Its name was Great Bear. There were about twenty or more rapid boats and they hired about fifteen to twenty pilots from Fort Franklin and Fort Norman. Francis Tatti was there, Joe Blondin, and Joe Saul were all pilots.

By 1937 or 1938 they had all the machinery in so there wasn't enough work for the two big boats and Hudson Bay pulled out.

When the war broke out the mine was closed and everybody was gone. But after two or three years, they must have found out that it was important and they opened it again.

We only had radio news here so we didn't know anything more about it. Later, we found out that the uranium was made into an atomic bomb which was dropped on the Japanese.

—Isadore Yukon

SIDEBAR: ABOUT "FIRST MACHINES" CHAPTER

IN THE EARLY DAYS, the Dene walked wherever they wanted to go. When the winter landscape was covered in ice and snow, they used snowshoes. Dogs and people pulled sleds. In spring, ice melted, and rivers and lakes opened up for canoes. Survival for the Dene meant being on the move, following the caribou, hunting, ice fishing, and in the summer, heading for their fishing camps. The Dene were at one with the land, knowing how to live in every season, in every place. Their knowledge was passed down through the generations in song and story. They knew their land so well that, as they journeyed throughout their vast territory, they were never lost. They knew where to find anything and everything they needed.

The Mackenzie River was the gateway for the Europeans into the North. The explorers, the missionaries, the fur traders, the prospectors and the miners came to open the North to exploit its resources; furs, gold, oil, uranium. Transportation and communication between settlements and the South were key for this to occur.

During the culture contact period, communication depended on mail, delivered by dog teams, or on foot. Later, steamboats would deliver mail in the summertime. But then the planes came.

Early flights were dangerous. There were few landing strips, so planes were provided with floats and skis. There were no maps except those hand-drawn so good guesses were important. The bush pilots flew through blizzards, tried and failed to take off in fog, suffered from frostbite and combatted darkness and subzero weather. Despite these limitations, planes were soon travelling throughout Canada's North, both winter and summer.

The first mail to come by air arrived in January 1929. Wop May, a famous World War pilot from southern Canada, was the first pilot to fly along the Arctic coastline, over the Barren Lands, as well as following the 3,218-kilometre length of the Mackenzie River. In 1930, Wop May flew the first prospectors into Great Bear Lake to locate the uranium that was subsequently used to make atomic bombs.

The Elders remember the first time the planes came and recount the exhilaration of a first flight, of owning a kicker, (the Evinrude outboard motor), and communication by radio. The stories recapture their fun and their humour. Thanks to the movie, *We Remember,* we can still hear them laughing, and can join in with them, sharing their joy. – *Sarah Stewart*

10. First Machines

Nakhwant geʔtr'oonahtan zheh

t'idich'uu daiʔ gwanoo , khaii juuk'anʔ ts'at candle iidiʔih. Joe Blondin.

"In our school days everything was
coal oil lamps and candles."

— Joe Blondin

Evinrude adapted for canoe by Dene.
Photo: CBC North.

Dene with Evinrudes on Mackenzie.
Photo: CBC.

Plane and dog team Eldorado Mine and Refining Ltd., Port Radium.
Photo: National Photography Collection Public Archives.

Bishop Breynat and his plane at the docks.
Photo: CBC.

Kickers

THE Mountain Indians, the Willow Lakers, the Whitefish Lakers, the Mackenzie River, and Franklin Indians all came in to Fort Norman in the spring for a while.

The Franklin people used to camp about thirty miles from the fort and my cousin, little Eddie Blondin, and I paddled down there with a three-horse kicker. That was my first ride with an outboard motor and I travelled with him all the way down to the camp. It took all that day.

Well you know how slow a three-horse kicker is! When we arrived at the camp, everybody wanted to tie their canoes together and have a ride to the fort. Over forty boats. There was quite a squabble about that. How's a three-horse kicker going to pull all that many!

—Joe Blondin

IN 1921 we lived in Aklavik and my uncle Kenneth Stewart had a little machine in the back of his skiff. We all came out of the tents and watched it.

He hired boys to cut logs to build the church in Aklavik and every day he took lunch up to them with the little Evinrude. Finally we got used to it.

—Sarah Simon

IN 1924 my brother was living here in Aklavik and I wanted to visit him. There was an Eskimo who came up to Fort McPherson and as he was going back there my dad asked if I could go with him. He had an inboard motor in his whaleboat and I really wanted to go in it. I did want to visit my brother all right, but how I wanted to ride in that boat!

—Jim Sittichinli

Gathering around the early radio.
Photo: Frame from the film We Remember.

Snarl of wires and big batteries to run the radio.
Photo: Frame from the film We Remember.

Headphones were needed to hear the occasional transmission.
Photo: Frame from the film We Remember.

Waiting for the static to bring in news of the day.
Photo: Frame from the film We Remember.

IN 1929 there was another trader here who was bringing in kickers. My father-in-law was an old man and he and his wife were camping with me at the fish camp.

Early in the morning I woke up and they were already up, sitting drinking tea. I heard him say to the old woman, "I visited that trader and he told me he's bringing in kickers!"

"What is that?" she said.

"The machine that pushes the boat around."

"So now our young people will run around with kickers. If they aren't careful, once it's broken, they won't know how to repair it."

"Do you know what ten-horse kicker means?"

"How can I know?"

"You remember in Dawson we saw one-horse kicker pull a great big heavy load on a wagon? Well this ten-horse kicker is as strong as ten horses."

"Oh!" she was so surprised. "But how big must the boat be for a machine that size?"

"You are not wise!" he said.

—Sarah Simon

THE Eskimos all had big schooners with two masts. They could go by wind down stream but coming up to Fort McPherson was hard until they got kickers.

—Sarah Simon

WE are staying at the fish camp when all at once we heard a kicker coming. We were told surveyors were coming and here they were surveying back and forth. Everybody was watching them.

—Sarah Simon

WHEN we were in school in Providence, the Bishop always came down by canoe with a kicker. He used to take us for a ride so I knew about kickers. The people down here had never seen one so they were very excited. Before, we used to go to Willow Lake with a track line kicker but when there was a kicker in the store Itse went and bought it. It was nine horse power. We used it to pull three boats.

The people were very pleased with it. The kicker worked for you.

—Elizabeth Yakeleya

Planes

BISHOP BREYNAT had a plane and travelled through the Mackenzie District spending three or four days in each settlement. One day, it was a Sunday, in Fort Norman, we asked the pilot, Bisson, if we could have a ride.

"Well somebody has to pay for the gas." he said and charged us three dollars.

I went on the third trip and sat in the co-pilot's seat. Fred Andrew was sitting right behind me. It was a nice sunshiny day and we went up high. Then Fred Andrew put his mouth alongside my ear and said, "Can you ask the pilot to do some tricks, you know stunts?"

So I asked and the next thing the pilot shut the engine off and we were heading straight for the Mackenzie. I thought my guts were coming out of my nose!

Fred grabbed my ears from behind and put both feet on the back of the chair. He just about tore my head off. Everybody was hanging on and screaming.

When we landed back at Norman, Fred was as white as a sheet of paper. We all were and that's the honest truth.

—Joe Blondin

THE Evinrudes cost fifty dollars and make a lot of noise. The people didn't like them because they hadn't enough power to pull two canoes and so one canoe would always be way ahead. The people preferred to paddle. The next Evinrude that came was much better.

—*John Blondin*

THE first time I saw a plane I thought it was maybe an eagle hanging onto something. There was confusion with people running in all directions. Of course when you're a kid you want to see everything. I was more excited than scared.

—*Joe Blondin*

OH, more than sixty years ago I saw the plane for the first time. The white man had told a few of the boys about the plane.

"I wish I could see one!" I said.

"You will later on. You'll see lots."

You know how the tail is on a plane? Well when the first plane came somebody said, "Look at that! Somebody is standing on behind." That made us laugh!

—*Peter Thompson*

In 1920 I was in Hay River School when I saw two planes. The principal was a minister and he must have had a radio because he told us a plane was coming. Lots of people were scared of it and ran into the bush. The first plane came on pontoons.

—*Jim Sittichinli*

We heard in Simpson on the radio that there would be a plane the following day. Everyone was so excited and wanted to see it. It was a clear day. The sun was shining when we heard something coming. It sounded like thunder. Some people were scared and ran inside. It was going so fast we thought it was going to crash when it hit the water. The nose went right up. The next year the Bishop had a plane and let everyone have a ride. When the pilot dived down close to the lake the people yelled their heads off. The pilot just laughed.

—John Blondin

I saw a plane when I was in school in Providence. We were in church saying our rosary when we heard something fly over the top. One sister went out and told the father who was saying prayers. After we went back to our rooms, she said, "The airplane has come. If you are good, you will see it. If you are bad you won't." The next day we all went to see it.

—Elizabeth Yakeleya

All at once we heard the cry, "Airplane! Airplane!" We ran outside, children hanging on to us they are so scared. It looked like a mosquito hawk and it was coming closer and closer. I was running, looking for my children, when I saw the plane right overhead. I ran and hid behind a barge until the plane landed. Indians, Eskimos and white people all ran to the shore to see it.

I saw my girls hanging on to a white man. They ran to me and I hung on to them. The door of the plane opened and two men came out.

"Mom, are those men alright? They're not going to kill us?"

"No, no, they're good people."

That's the first time I saw a plane.

—Sarah Simon

Radio

WE first heard the radio in 1926 or 1927 at Hay River School. William Firth, the manager of Hudson Bay had a radio too. William Firth and I listened to his. You had to use earphones and we all took it in turns.

I was very surprised to hear what came out of that music box. (That's what we called it.) Sometimes it was just static and that just about burst your ears! I wouldn't listen at first because I am too greedy of my hearing!

In 1940 we had broadcasts of the church service on Sundays in English, Loucheux, and Eskimo from the radio, a station in Aklavik. If there was no missionary, everybody came into the tent and listened to it.

People couldn't understand how the radio worked at first. One woman had heard on the radio that her cousin had died so she went to tell her mother.

"Mother, I have news for you. It said on the radio that Peter Alexie had died."

"Get out of this tent!" she cried, "I don't like that machine gossiping."

Once I had a radio message to pass on to an old woman from her daughter. When I told her she said, "Oh go on! How can a machine talk?"

Another woman spoke to her. "Look here Ellen, you have to believe what our granddaughter says. We had better not talk about other people anymore or that machine will tell them. We had better be good grandmothers to our grandchildren."

These are just the old people's ideas, I know that!

— Sarah Simon

Electricity

Nobody had seen electric lights before. My cousin Joe Kenny and me went up to Hudson Bay and the cook for the radio station, Jack Hardy, asked us to come in and have coffee. So we stayed until it was getting late.

One of the Royal Signal Corps came in and put his finger on the wall. Everything just lit up! Joe got so excited he shouted, "The devil must be helping that guy. He just poked his finger on the wall and look at that!"

In our school days everything was coal oil lamps and candles.

—Joe Blondin

In 1974 my wife and I went to Ottawa to get the Order of Canada which I was awarded because I began the Hamlet of Fort Franklin. I had been to Tuktoyaktuk and Baffin Island to learn how settlement councils worked all in my own time.

My wife had never seen a city before and she was scared of all the people. I couldn't leave her. She'd never seen an escalator or self-serve restaurant or automatic doors before. Up here you know you walk ahead and the women walk behind you but down in the city, you can't do that!

She stood on the rug at the airport and the doors opened. She looked around, "Who opened the doors?"

—Isadore Yukon

SIDEBAR: ABOUT "THE MAD TRAPPER" CHAPTER

Nobody knows who Albert Johnson really was or where he came from but his exploits in the Mackenzie Mountains have made him a part of Canadian folk lore. In 1931 he came North on a raft with $3,000 in his pocket and rigged himself out for a winter's trapping at the bay in Fort McPherson. After he had asked for mail in the name of Albert Johnson, he went down Rat River and built a cabin.

The RCMP followed him there later to investigate complaints that he was springing traps. They were unable to get inside the cabin. The RCMP tried unsuccessfully on three more occasions to get Johnson out of his cabin or to get inside. In the process one man was wounded.

It was the middle of winter and the temperature plummeted. Nobody was able to sustain a siege outside for any length of time. The last time the police came back Johnson was gone.

For six weeks he successfully evaded capture as he fled over rugged terrain, without shelter, in temperatures, of –30 degrees C and colder, hunting to live while he himself was hunted. He threw the pursuers off his trail by doubling back and walking in their tracks, or reversing his snowshoes. He camped by day without a fire and travelled by night.

The only time the patrol got close, one man was killed, another wounded.

He had crossed over the mountains, an amazing feat under such conditions. Johnson was on his way to Alaska and freedom when a plane, flown by Wop May, joined the search party.

Johnson, "The Mad Trapper," was caught out in the open with nowhere to hide. He buried himself half in the snow and took cover behind his packsack. He was shot to death.

– *Sarah Stewart*

11. The Mad Trapper

Akoo diinihdhan, Albert Johnson gwiizii gwitr'it t'agwahʔih kwah, zhat k'aheedik gwitshih. Niveh t'ahʔii anaajat. Dinjii nizii jiʔ, juu nahʔii ts'at giheekhyah gwid akoo dinuh kwah. Andrew Kunnizzi.

"I think Albert Johnson had done some
bad work before he came here."

— Andrew Kunnizzi

RCMP Commemorative medal celebrating the capture of The Mad Trapper.

I WAS the first man to talk to Albert Johnson. He had pitched his tent about a mile or two from Fort McPherson and tied up his little raft that he built up on the Peel River. We went up there with kickers to see him. I walked up the bank and said, "Hello." He said, "Hello."

The mosquitoes were pretty bad and he fixed up leaves so you couldn't go in the tent where he was.

I said, "What's your name?" He said, "Albert Johnson."

"Where do you come from?" I asked.

I can't remember what he said. It was either Rat or Red River.

"Where are you going?" He lifted up the tent and all I saw of him was just one eye.

"Don't bother me!" he said.

We went back to the boat and headed off. Later he went into Fort McPherson.

—Andrew Kunnizzi

ALBERT JOHNSON was a tall man, bent over a little bit. When he came to Fort McPherson, he bought a canoe off Abraham Francis and paddled down the river.

I had a fish camp down there and I saw him go by. After a few days I saw him come back. I told my wife to cook for him so we could give him something to eat. But he paddled by on the other side of the river and didn't stop at all.

The first creek he got to was Husky River and he paddled up there. It was getting cold then so he decided to build a cabin and it was after that the trouble began.

William Snowshoe went up that way, that was his trapline. He didn't know that man was there, he didn't see him. But he did see lynx traps set. He went along and set his own traps. When he went to see his traps later he saw they had been sprung and hung up in the trees. He didn't know what it was all about so he went and reported it.

I was one of the searchers and went to Johnson's cabin. It wasn't like cabins are. His was built of big logs put on the ground and in between the logs he had dug into the ground and that was where he had his bed. It was all caved in and we couldn't see. They tried to shine a flashlight in where he was but Johnson shot it right out of the man's hand. That's how I knew he was a good shooter.

I was away searching for him for twelve days. I never saw him once. Later on, some families were travelling up that way and that was when I met the inspector again. He told me to go with him, but I had to refuse as I had to hunt for my family. So while I was there with my family was when they caught him.

Johnson was a good shot and he really knew how to set traps. I saw them and he knew what he was doing. I don't think he was a good man because of how he been doing things like that before we ever met him.

—Johnny Kaye

I THINK Albert Johnson had done some bad work in another place before he came here. He was scared of the police. If he was a good man, he would have talked to people. But he would not talk to anyone.

—Andrew Kunnizzi

SIDEBAR: ABOUT "CANOL ROAD" CHAPTER

CANOL ROAD was built so a pipeline could be laid to carry oil from Norman Wells to Whitehorse where it would be refined. The oil was to supply the US Army defending Alaska against the expected Japanese invasion.

The pipeline, begun in 1942, was completed in 1943 and abandoned the same year. The threat of invasion was over. The pipeline was left to rust and Canol Road returned to bush.

– Sarah Stewart

12. *Canol Road*

"jadee nakhwozheh giɔdeɔdinohtin." Akoo

dugwahntshii łoo giinzuh kwah. Elizabeth Yakelaya

"Why have you locked yourselves in the houses?
They're not as bad as all that!"

— *Elizabeth Yakeleya*

Americans arrive to work on Canol Road.
Photo: Prince of Wales Northern Heritage Centre, Yellowknife.

WHEN the Canol Road was in full swing we lived below the camp one winter. It was quite a place. All the buildings were made like igloos and there were all kinds of people there. That was the first time I saw a black person.

We used to drive up there on Sunday on our dog team to see what was going on. My husband used to put us all on the sleigh with a blanket.

—*Mary Wilson*

Canol Road left to rust.
Photo: Prince of Wales Northern Heritage Centre, Yellowknife.

THE MAN from [Hudson] Bay told us that *The Distributor* was coming and that we would see lots of Americans. We heard before that those men would take the women away from their husbands.

Aunt Mary, Phoebe, her sister and myself were in our house when we heard *The Distributor* was coming. We locked the doors and closed the curtains. Grandfather ran outside with the men, there were no women.

We opened the curtains, looked out and saw black people for the first time. We were scared. Grandfather was talking to Fred Berens who called out, "Why have you locked yourselves in the houses? They're not as bad as all that!"

—*Elizabeth Yakeleya*

ABOUT "MACKENZIE VALLEY PIPELINE" CHAPTER

FROM 1975 to 1976, Mr. Justice Thomas R. Berger was appointed by the Privy Council to form an Inquiry into and to report on the conditions that should be imposed on the building of a pipeline to transport gas from the Beaufort Sea, down the Mackenzie Valley into Alberta. The Berger Inquiry travelled to every community in the Mackenzie Valley and to cities across Canada to listen to people's concerns and opinions. It was at stops in Aklavik, Fort Good Hope, Fort McPherson, Fort Simpson, Fort Norman, and Norman Wells that Justice Berger was met with these words:*

> Chief Fred Greenland said to the Inquiry at Aklavik:
> It's clear to me what the Native People are saying today. They're discussing not their future but the future of their children and grandchildren, and if the Government continues to refuse or neglect [us] ... I think the natives would just stop their effort and discussions and the opportunities for a peaceful settlement would be lost. We must choose wisely and carefully because there will be a future generation of Canadians who will live with the results.

> Frank T'Seleie, Chief at Fort Good Hope told the Inquiry:
> It is for this unborn child, Mr. Berger, that my nation will stop the pipeline. It is so that this unborn child can know the freedom of this land that I would be willing to lay down my life.

* Published in "Northern Frontier, Northern Homeland: The Report of the Mackenzie Valley Pipeline Inquiry" Volume 1. By Justice Thomas R. Berger. Minister of Supply and Services Canada, 1977.

Philip Blake told the Inquiry at Fort McPherson:

If your nation chooses ... to continue to try and destroy our nation, then I hope you will understand why we are willing to fight so that our nation can survive. It is our world. We do not wish to push our world onto you. But we are willing to defend it for ourselves, our children, and our grandchildren. If your nation becomes so violent that it would tear up our land, destroy our society and our future, and occupy our homeland, by trying to impose this pipeline against our will, then of course we will have no choice but to react with violence. I hope we do not have to do that. For it is not the way we would choose. However, if we are forced to blow up the pipeline ... I hope you will not only look on the violence of Indian action, but also on the violence of your own nation which would force us to take such a course. We will never initiate violence. But if your nation threatens by its own violent action to destroy our nation, you will have given us no choice. Please do not force us into this position. For we would all lose too much.

Chief Jim Antoine of Fort Simpson:

... every time we try to do something, within the system ... it doesn't seem to work for us, as Indian people. We tried it, we tried to use it, it doesn't work for us.... We're going to keep on trying to use the system until we get frustrated enough that we're going to try changing it. I think that's where it's directed, that's where it's going. I would stand with my brother from Good Hope that he would lay down his life for what he believes in, and I feel the same way.

Mr. Justice Thomas R. Berger responded to Indigenous concerns with a statement seen and heard in the NFB film *Fort Good Hope* by Ron Orieux:*

> We have an assumption our technology can do anything. The Native Peoples of the North – the Indians, the Métis, the Inuit ... we have a tendency to assume that nothing that they say can make a difference, that nothing they say about the environment can contribute in any way to the wealth of knowledge we've accumulated in scientific surveys and research. We think that our engineering and science and technology is supreme. The fact is that people all over the world are telling those of us who live in North America, "You people are using more than your fair share of the world's energy and resources." Here (in the North), we have people within the boundaries of our own country saying to us, "You're using more than your fair share of the energy and resources that exist."

Partly because the environmental impact of the pipeline would seriously threaten the Dene way of life, Justice Berger recommended that there be a ten-year moratorium on development in the North. The Mackenzie Valley Pipeline has never been built.

– Lorene Shyba

* From an interview with Justice Thomas R. Berger in the documentary *Fort Good Hope.* Directed by Ron Orieux. 1977 National Film Board of Canada.

13. *Mackenzie Valley Pipeline*

Akoo dehihnjah, k'eejit kat gwiizii gik'inoonjih, yeendoo gweedhaa geenjit gwik'itedziihohɂeh. Jim Sittichinli.

"Try to understand the changes going on today!
Be prepared for the future."

— John Blondin

Nugwidadhat srii t'igwinaanch'uu gwinoo, dinjii tshid nilii, akoo diginuh. Nakhwanan zhit iitsii gwizhaa tr'iheetthał. Gwid gat'igwiiniidhan kwah. Nakhwanan t'iinch'uh. Vakak nakhwogoonlii, gwizhit adigwidjaandaii. Aii iitsii gwizhah k'iighe› gweheekwaa. Juk drin aii gwizhit gwiidindaii. Berger nugwidadhat neekaii gwizhit iitsii gwizhah eenjit gwitr'it t'ugwah›in. Duuyeh ganałdeh. Gwiinleii gik'inilnjik, judin zhuu k'eejit kat gwik'iighe› gahgidindaii ji›. Akoo diinihdhan, Canada gwizhit dinjii zhuh kat, eenjit gahgwidindaii goodlit daganan eenjit kheenjit duk t'igiinch'uh giinlih. Gold chan ts'at khaii hah ge›dinditin, dinjii kat gwiizii gahgidindaih kwah, gwid oonjit aii gahdindaih. Tshid nilii hah srigwinlik, chan akoo dugwidi›ih ji› nakhwant geenjit ninji›iidadhat. Nakhwonan kat gwitch'in iidilii. Akoo dehihnjah, k'eejit kat gwiizii gik'inoonjih, yeendoo gweedhaa geenjit gwik'itedziihoh›eh. Jim Sittichinli.

R to L. Louie Blondin, Whit Fraser, Jim Edwards Sittichinli, Joe Toby at the Berger Inquiry, Yellowknife.
Photo: Native Communications Society NWT.

A FEW years ago, the Government said they were going to build a pipeline on our land but nobody wanted that. The land is how we make our living. The pipeline would do a lot of damage, chase away the animals which people still depend on today. The fur will be destroyed by the pipeline.

I worked with Berger for two and a half years on the Pipeline Inquiry. It was something I'll never forget. It made me understand many things. I hope the Inquiry will help the young people. I think it did something for all Native people across Canada. It made them understand how they should care for their land and helped them to be proud of themselves.

When the gold and oil opened up the people didn't know too much but the white man knew lots. He went ahead and made an agreement with the Government. If anything ever happens like that again, we want to be the ones making the agreement.

We are the people of the land. I would say to my young people, "Try to understand the changes going on today! Be prepared for the future."

— *Jim Sittichinli*

Elder Marie Blondin and Raymond Yakeleya at Berger Inquiry. Norman Wells, Northwest Territories, 1975.

Raymond Yakeleya
Speaking at Norman Wells
to the Berger Inquiry*

Our backs are turned to the corners.
This is our last stand.
I ask each and every one of you in this room,
What would you do if you were in our shoes?
How would you feel
If you had these conditions on you?

I ask you one more time, let us negotiate,
There's still time, but don't force us.
Because this time we have nothing to lose.
When I ask for
The lives of my people,
Am I asking you for too much?

We admit that we are fearful,
But to be fearful is not to be without courage.
We admit that we are distrustful,
But we are not without wisdom in seeking harmony.

— Raymond Yakeleya

* Published in "Northern Frontier, Northern Homeland: The Report of the Mackenzie Valley Pipeline Inquiry" Volume 1. By Justice Thomas R. Berger. Minister of Supply and Services Canada, 1977.

Elder Elizabeth Yakeleya.
Painting: Deborah Demarais.

14. *Time of Change*

Akoo duuleh k'eejit duguuvałnuh. Nakhwotsuu oodhodhohch'eii. Nakhwotiʔ guuk'it gwitr'it t'igohʔih. Duuleh akoo duguuvałnuh, nits'oo gwiinzii gugweheedindaii eenjit. Elizabeth Yakelaya.

"I would tell my young people listen to their granny,
listen to their father and follow their examples.
I would tell them a story about how to live
and if they listened, they would live long."

— *Elizabeth Yakeleya*

Dene Drum Dance.
Photo: Native Communications Society NWT.

Young Dene at a drum dance.
Photo: Native Communications Society NWT.

WHEN I was growing up, I lived on the Hudson Bay lot. We had our own house at the back. Later on, all the People had their own log houses, nice houses. I have pictures on the lantern slides. The Government built new houses in 1966. They didn't even ask the poor man where he wanted his house. It was just, "That's your house. Go in there!" Even though there were still good log houses that they could have stayed in.

—Sarah Simon

AS soon as they began building houses for the people they never asked where we would like our homes. They just went ahead, built wherever they wanted. Put us anywhere. If we complained they never recognized us, just listened and that was all. If I want to build a house on this land, my land, I have to pay for a lot before I can do that. I had my own log house but the Government said I had to move into a Government house and I would have to pay rent. So I moved and now I have to pay rent.

—Johnny Kaye

THE People go to school and learn white man's ways and don't know about the old ways. They don't listen to the old people who know how to live off the country. The young people stay in town and always ask the old people for money. That's not the way to live.

—Andrew Kunnizzi

LIFE in the bush was sometimes pretty hard but it sure was a good life. The people were so happy. Now I have a house and I just sit down and turn the switch and it gets as warm as I want. I don't like that. I'd rather cut the wood and haul it myself. That's why I didn't rent a house for a very long time but my daughter and son persuaded me. Now I've got nothing to do. I just sit down.

—Andrew Kunnizzi

NOWADAYS children go to school. The government says, "Put your children in school and if they stay long enough they'll come back as nurses, doctors, and teachers and secretaries."

We don't see that.

I want to see my young people well educated but there is nothing much for them to do. Some still have the chance to live on the land. Young children should have a chance to live in their own country.

Young boys and girls get an education then come back to Fort McPherson. There's nothing to do. They behave and try to do their best but soon they get bored. If they ask for a job it takes such a long time. They give up hope, still, there's lots of goodness in the young people.

—Sarah Simon

I HAVE one young grandson. I'd sooner have him in the bush than going to school, I want him to be a bushman like me. That's what I did for the school for two winters. I took the kids out and taught them how to trap beaver, how to fish and hunt. Everything.

—Isadore Yukon

I WENT to school. All I had was grade 4. It's only now that the People are beginning to understand about education. But they can only go to grade 9 and then they have to leave home for further grades. The young people don't like to leave their homeland and when they're taken away, they don't want to learn. The People think they would like the young people educated in their own communities. I'd like to see the young people becoming teachers. Most of our teachers come from outside of the North and teach the children white man's ways only and not about the land.

— Jim Sittichinli

THE People are losing their language. Every day I'm talking about that to my People. I know it's no good for them.

—Sarah Simon

WHEN I came back from school in 1933, all we ever spoke was Slavey. It's just recently, since the kids started going to the hostels, that's when the language was just dropped. Even mothers who never went to school and never spoke English before learn it from their kids and speak it with them. I worry a lot about the kids in Good Hope, my hometown.

All the little ones speak in English. Now they are teaching it in the school, but how much can a school accomplish if parents aren't helping? In the schools they have started to teach Dene language but it's only for part of the day and just the basics such as what do you call a cup, pencil, not how to carry on a conversation. The only way we can preserve the language is by the parents teaching the children at home as well as them learning at school.

I don't think it is too late. People are becoming aware and realize what is happening. They are discussing it in the Legislative Assembly and people in the communities are working on how to write our language down.

—Mary Wilson

NOWADAYS some of the young people don't even know how to chop their own wood. I would like the children to go to school until grade 7 and then they should stay home and go in the bush for two or three years to learn, then they could go back and finish their grades. So they would know white man's ways and Indian ways. Then they are equal.

—Elizabeth Yakeleya

THE young people go to school but they don't use their education because of alcohol. It is so plentiful and it is getting worse all the time. It's spoiling the people. I would be glad if there was no liquor, if they stopped it coming in.

—Johnny Kaye

MANY bad things come from alcohol. We lose too many good people. We lose track of good relationships.

—Sarah Simon

WHEN I was growing up, there was no whisky in town but now the people are bad for drinking. In the winter one boy shot himself. He was drunk. I want to tell my young people, "Quit drinking! Don't drink!"

—Peter Thompson

THE life that we had before the white people came here was a good life. There was no sickness and we never talked about the future or worried about money.

There was no drinking except tea and some of the people didn't even have that. I was 26 before I had tea!

We enjoyed ourselves when we met together in the spring and at Christmas but today it is different. People drink and get mad at each other. Some are drowned, or are in a fire, or freeze to death. It happens all the time. That is no life. No life at all.

A person loses himself in drink. He doesn't know who he is anymore and doesn't know what kind of life he wants. Some young people don't use their money well, don't keep it for hard times. They spend it right away. On what? On liquor. If they get married and do that, the poor children will starve.

I saw an Indian camp and the mother and father were drunk. There were little boys and girls and they looked in the cupboards for food. There was nothing. They sneaked out to another house but the door was locked. They got in through the window and found some flour. They were so hungry that they ate it just like that. There was a foot of snow on the ground.

That is misery.

—John Blondin

I THINK the drinking spoils the young people. I wish the Government would cut it right out. Whenever they get a bit of money, people buy whiskey, not even grub. That makes me sick. The Government sells it or the bootlegger brings it in here for twenty-five or thirty dollars a bottle. They still pay. The Government makes a big mistake. If they cut it out they will help the people. They might go hunting and trapping. Quite a few times they asked the Government to cut it out but they still make money selling it.

We can't do anything about it.

—Andrew Kunnizzi

ONE of the happiest times of my life was when my kids were small. My first husband loved the children so much and we got along real good together. That was before alcohol came to the North and we didn't have too much to worry about. Life was simple but it was happy.

Since alcohol came the people changed and nothing is the same anymore.

I had a part of it myself. I was one of the lucky ones and realized what was happening to me. I asked myself, "Where is it going to end?"

I got scared and started looking for help. You have to have a strong desire to change and go back to the kind of person you used to be. A lot of suffering is involved.

It's been thirteen years since I made up my mind it was time to turn around. I found people ready to help me and thank God I hung on. You can't tell a person to quit. He won't unless he wants to himself. Only when he starts to see himself for what he is, sees what he is doing to himself and his loved ones, can he change.

The happiest time in my life was when I finally found the way back to the life I had before. I used to be afraid of people and think everybody talked about me and looked down on me. I carried all this guilt and hated myself. Such a lonely life.

You have to go through that suffering yourself to be able to understand the people. I see them going through that day after day when I come home from work. It hurts me so much I wish I could help. How do they feel? I felt just caged in, nowhere to turn to, no way out. Sometimes when I look back, I think I'm glad it happened to me. It made me a different person. I look at the whole world differently.

I appreciate little things that one time I never cared about. In spring when the sun shines, all is nice and

Children in Dene language class.
Photo: Frame from the film We Remember.

quiet, you feel light inside. There is no block like you carried around at one time.

A year after that we moved back to Good Hope. There's a little river there, the Rabbit Skin River, and it's a good fishing place. On Sunday we went there in our canoe and my husband caught a real nice big fish. We stopped on a nice beach and my husband went for a walk in the bush while I was cooking.

There was no wind, not a sound but the water flowing and the fire burning. It was so peaceful. Sunday mornings had been my worst time when I was drinking. The water, nature — it hit me. How grateful I was to be back to that kind of life. I bowed my head and said a prayer.

—Mary Wilson

A FEW older women are tanning moose skin and making babiche and other things. After they are gone who is going to do it? I am very glad and pleased younger women are taking over. Many of them are trying now. Some of the young families move up to live off the land for the winter. They haven't done that for a long time. They began to realize our way of life is dying. They are trying to make it live again.

—Sarah Simon

I would tell my young people listen to their granny, listen to their father and follow their examples. I would tell them a story about how to live and if they listened, they would live long.

—Elizabeth Yakeleya

WE always help each other. You can't be a man all the time. If I help you now, then when I am stuck you will remember me and help me.

But it is not like that anymore.

—John Blondin

I WOULD tell my young people, " Quit your drinking and start living the life your parents lived. Get in training, use your education and become a teacher or nurse. Not only white people were made for that. Indian too."

—Sarah Simon

I DON'T want to be young again. I used my young days well and did all that I wanted to do.

My own people here have named their community hall after me and my portrait hangs there. I thank my people for doing that for me so I will be remembered.

—Johnny Kaye

When I was ten years old, I knew how to live in the bush. I knew how to hunt, fish, set snares and make an arrow to get a chicken. We had to make snowshoes and toboggans. We needed them for survival. When we make something for the first time, it's no good but the second one is better. After ten attempts they say, "Okay Now you know how to make that." Then we laugh we are so happy.

When the young people are stuck who will give them snowshoes? They don't know how to hunt. They can't eat grass. How will they make moccasins? The people now are like green grass. They don't know a thing. They don't even know how to tan a moose hide. Today they depend on white people.

But maybe our life will change again. We don't know. We have to keep this knowledge for our children. My grandfather taught me and I really thank him for that. I made a good life for myself. I hope the young generation will have the same.

—John Blondin

Starlight Cutter. Antoine Mountain.

Winter is a time of
staying indoors for much of the day.
For that you always need a
steady supply of good, dry wood.
—Antoine

Part III

Stories from the People

Leanne Goose

Antoine Mountain

Raymond Yakeleya

George Blondin

Tutichak

Leanne Goose

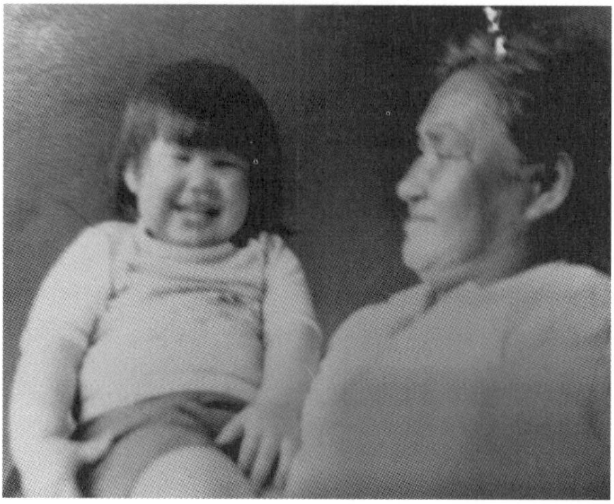

Baby Leanne Goose with Nanak.

I DON'T REMEMBER the first time I slept here, but I do remember many mornings. The house made of hard work and sacrifice from the remnants of a Bombardier caboose, nothing is wasted here. Handmade eiderdown blankets, covered in paisley-patterned heavy woven cotton bury me in comfort. The sound of dishes clanging in the kitchen, the smell of oil and sourdough sizzling in a pan and her big voice.

"Tutichak, come and eat my Bunnik!" calls Nanak. I lie wrapped up in the linen cloud which must be what heaven feels like. I am nestled at the foot of Nanak's bed and lingering in the knowing that all this noise, all this hustle is just for me. If I wait a little longer, she will come and get me. I can hear her shuffled steps and the sound of the hide on the soles of her gowaks as she walks into the room. Her face is now close to mine, and she gestures for a hug. I wrap my arms tightly around her neck as if it were the last and she squeezes me tightly around my little waist. I sit on the edge of the bed and she tells me to give her my foot. I stick my little toes close to her nose, she leans in as if she is about the bite them. In the game we play, one by one, she slips on my socks, then a duffle and my little gowaks that look just like hers. I know that Nanak is here just for me.

I am thirsty and take my 'baba' in my teeth and walk into the brightness of the big room. Dadak is sitting at his work bench, crafted with silver corner caps over perfectly crafted wood. Dadak likes to make stuff from other stuff, he made this house. Dadak is cleaning shiny things with lots of tiny pieces spread across his worktable. I walk over to investigate but before my chubby fingers reach the polished metal he grumbles, "Aagh! Don't touch!" I give him glaring eyes, touch it anyway knocking the part to the floor and I run to stand behind Nanak.

Dadak says, "Come back here, help me find it."

I don't want to and find myself following the seam on her slacks with my finger and the creases at her knees. She picks me up and tells me, "qain," and a warm, soapy soft cloth covers my face and begins to rub off the layers of chocolate, snot and dirt. Last night I found, under the bed, a bag of chocolate and mints saved for Sunday visitors, but I know she secretly keeps the bag for me.

"Nakin qaivit?"

I point to her and she lets go a hearty laugh. I am squirming to run away as the cloth is rubbing my skin off I'm sure, but I see my breakfast at the table. Oh my favourite! Cranberries and cream, sourdough silver-dollar-sized pancakes and a new 'baba' filled with root beer. The radio is on and there is a man with an accent telling a story.

I try to listen, but the sound of his voice is so boring, yet it doesn't stop her from telling me, "Niparin!" But no one is shouting or laughing on the radio. Why do I have to be quiet? I continue to play with my spoon trying to pick up a piece of pancake and balance it so carefully towards my mouth. I miss, and the sticky pancake covered in corn syrup sticks to my belly and slides down to rest on my chubby leg. I pick it up and stuff into my mouth.

"Mmm, mamak!" Smiling,

humming a melody that is familiar only to me, I stand on the chair to find my berries and cream. A song comes on the radio and I can feel myself moving to the beat when it happens. The sound of glass crashing to the floor and a hand on my shoulder braces me from the carnage. The shrill sound of my own voice scares me, and my heart is broken. Root beer and glass cascade across the new linoleum floor. Dadak just fixed the new linoleum floor after the last flood and he is first to jump up to assess the damage.

He smiles at me and says, "Oh, no more baba now."

I cry harder now, lamenting over the loss of my dear baba. My face is wet with big tears, the taste of salt on my lips, and while they begin cleaning the broken pieces of my heart off the floor, a giant snot bubble bursts from my nose and Nanak begins to laugh. She laughs so hard that she is shaking, and I can't tell if she too is crying so I cry harder. Afraid that she may shatter onto the floor too. During this whole time, no one is holding me. No one dares to pick me up and tell me it's going to be okay. I hear a sound, someone is coming.

"Ataa!" I say and she repeats, "Ataa!"

The door opens, and the tears stop as Angaga comes inside and says, "Why come you cry Babing?" I stretch out my arms to him as he carefully sidesteps the carnage at his feet. He is smiling, and a slight giggle escapes his mouth, which makes me angry. My arms retract, and I can feel the whining rumbling over my tongue.

He tells me, "Don't be like that Babing, Anagaga loves you." I can feel his whiskers tickle my neck and shoulder and his long hair covers my sticky face. He lifts me up to hold me tight and I hug him and tight as I can.

He says, "No more baba now, Babing!"

How dare he! I shout, "*No!*" and glare at him with the meanest eyes. He laughs at me, harder than before.

He whispers in my ear, "No more baby now, you're a big girl. Don't need that stinky baba." I can feel my body shuddering at the thought and through heavy sighs, the crying starts again. I see her sweeping the broken pieces on to the cardboard with a goose wing broom and hear

Young Leanne Goose at Nanak and Dadak's.

the sound of glass pieces falling to the bottom of the metal can. Angaga puts me down back on the chair. The smell of Pine-Sol and bleach fill the room as she washes the sticky remnants off the new floor. Dadak is standing over, watching that his new floor isn't scratched, like a somber pallbearer at a funeral.

"Agh, this kit'! My shirt and jacket are sticky now!" Angaga declares. Nanak pauses from wringing out the strings of the grey mop to pass him a washcloth and starts to rub it on Angaga's brown snap-button shirt. I always thought he was so stylish, wearing clothes from the Simpsons-Sears catalogue—the same one with all the fancy toys.

He turns to look at me and says, "Ha-ha, no more baby now ah!" I stick out my tongue at him. Dadak just gave me a whole can of root-beer and I am playing with the tiny top hole pushed through to the inside of the can and I can hear the bubbles inside. I never got to have a whole can before, only in my baba. I feel proud and my cheeks are filled with root beer.

I hear her say to Angaga, "Sonny, fill up the washer, I will clean your clothes. Gee!" He looks at me and pinches my cheeks and root beer sprays him in the face.

"Agh, this kit', so damn rotten-*cute*!" and he begins to haul water to fill that big noisy wash tub.

Finally, Nanak is mine again and comes to me with a hand behind her back. I know she has something special for me, she always does. I let her put me on her lap and she has a new warm, soapy cloth wiping away the tears, the snot, the sticky syrup, the root beer to leave me with the memory of her hard-working hands and the sound of her voice, "Ahh, Tutichak, you are a big girl now ah!" I reach to touch her face and say, "Mine Nanak," and cuddle into that safe space against her breast, in her arms where I was her baby.

I wasn't there when she died but she came to me. I still hear her big voice bound in mine. When Dadak died, I sang to him as he drifted away knowing I was ready to be a big girl; hardworking, meticulous and free.

Words in Inuvialuktun

Tutichak — Grandchild *(too-ti-chāk)*
Nanak — Grandmother
Bunnik — Girl, daughter
Gowaks — Embroidered stroud on moose hide shoes *(gow-aks)*
Dadak — Grandfather
Qain — Come *(kine)*
Nakin qaivit? — Where did you come from? *(nakin kī vit)*
Niparin — Be quiet! *(Ne par īn)*
Mamak — Tastes good! *(maa maak)*
Ataa! — Shh, listen
Babing — Inuvialuktun/English slang for my baby *(babe ing)*
Angaga — Uncle *(Ána gaga)*
Gee— Hurry up, do it! *(hard g sound)*

How the Muskrat Created the World

Antoine Mountain *with Maurice Mendo*

Photo: Antoine Mountain

Maurice Mendo in front of the Muskrat mural in Tulita, NWT.

NO ONE can tell our old-time stories like an Elder can. When I was in Tulita in 2012 for my final summer of Sahtú in the Arts, an arts co-op program initiated by the Northwest Territories Government, I spent a good deal of my time with Elder Maurice Mendo. Since we are both Mountain Dene and closely related, we shared a common sense of humour, and we were close. I broached the idea of creating a mural for the new swimming pool in town, with a story involving our animal relatives. We eventually settled on "How Muskrat Created the World," the Dene creation story. Maurice was a born storyteller, but he had an added talent—he knew the traditional way of acting out all the parts of the story, including some absolutely lifelike imitations of the foibles and noble deeds of D'se (Muskrat). As he told it:

"All the animals were marooned on a large wooden raft, adrift on a flooded sea, trying to figure out a way to put the world they knew back together again. The only way to do so would be to send their best diver down to the bottom of the ocean and come back with even a bit of dirt, so they could rebuild the world.

"Loon volunteered, but it was decided even she could not do this impossible feat. Instead, Otter took his dive and was gone for some time. When he did come back up, he had failed.

"Next to go was Beaver, known for his way of dropping right straight down, sinking like a heavy boulder. Even he came back with naught to accomplish the task of creating the world anew.

"Finally, Muskrat piped up and was brave enough to volunteer to make his descent to the bottom. At this, all the animals laughed, saying that if even their best swimmers could not come back with the earth then what chance did this measly creature have of success?

"While all of this was being debated, Muskrat simply disappeared with a sharp splash like a small stone falling from on high and was gone, it seemed, for all of eternity. There was nothing the rest could do but wait for his return.

"Which he finally did, miraculously popping back out of the surface of the sea and landing back on the raft. His poor lifeless body lay there, barely gasping for air.

"But when the rest of the Animal Nation checked his paws closely, there in a tight grip was just a bit of ground, maybe enough to create the land they needed so.

"They worked and laboured to make the world as they had loved it before. Wolf was sent forth to run and howl every now and again, so they would know the size of Mother Earth.

"When they were satisfied, they all turned and gave thanks to the mighty Muskrat for remaking this world we now live in."

The Slingshot and the Songbird

Raymond Yakeleya

SPRING ARRIVED with its warm yellow and pink sunlight on the face of Bear Rock Mountain, which watches over my hometown of Tulita, Northwest Territories. Noisy black, white, and grey snowbirds were flying everywhere. The snow was still on the ground, but we knew spring had arrived. The snow was soft. Icicles on the roof melted, making puddles of water and mud. Even the air smelled different, like it was cleaner. The Elders and babies sat outside enjoying themselves in the sun, with a small fire burning, creating smoke. A tea kettle perched on the fire for visitors — bannock too.

Life was good and simple then. We all went to a two-room schoolhouse to learn how to read and write. After school, my brothers and I would saw and chop wood, collect ice from the Mackenzie River for drinking water, for washing clothes, and for the weekly Saturday night bath. My sisters would help mother cook, bake bread and cinnamon buns, wash the dishes, and clean up the house. There was always something to do — no end to it.

We all did our homework by the light of the Coleman gas lamp and sometimes by the candle on the kitchen table. About this time, I got to read and know about Huckleberry Finn and Dennis the Menace and became an admirer of both of them. I liked Huckleberry Finn's adventures and his sense of righteousness. And Dennis the Menace was always on the not-so-innocent trail of mischief. Through books I got to know about the outside world where things were very different from what we knew in our isolated northern town of 300 people, 178 dogs, and one tomcat named Pinky. We knew about wolves, bears, and ptarmigans, and the northern lights.

Spring was everyone's favorite time. Easter holidays and no school for ten days was something to look forward to — better still, no homework. The trappers started to come in from their traplines with their dog teams. The dog harnesses would jingle from the bells and ribbons attached to them. We could hear them before we saw them. Then they came in from all directions, their blue, red and yellow ribbons flashing. Their sleds were filled with furs and their faces eager to see their families and friends. We would help them tie up and feed their dogs as they greeted everyone. Hugs, handshakes, smiles, kisses, and laughter everywhere. We knew there would be fiddle dances and drum dances soon when everyone got in safely. Excitement was in the air.

This was the time I would watch my older cousins and what they were doing. They would line up tin cans and empty bottles on the side of the roads and spend hours shooting rocks at them with their slingshots. They got to be very good marksmen, hitting almost everything they saw with one shot. The younger boys, including me, were envious and I decided in my mind that I would make the best slingshot and shoot like my older cousins and friends.

I spent days and hours looking for the right willow tree that had just the perfect Y-shaped branches. They had to be straight, of equal thickness, and not too wide. This was one of the most important parts of the slingshot, good wood and no knots.

I found just such a willow tree on Granny's rabbit-snaring trail on the high riverbank. I took my mom's kitchen cutting knife and spent many hours, happily shaping my slingshot. I was careful not to cut too much away. I took my time. I wanted it to be the best. It was the first time I made a slingshot, so I was proud of what I was doing.

We did not have any cars in my hometown, but we had three trucks. The trucks drove on tires that had inflatable inner tubes and when the tires wore out, the owners would get rid of them at the dump, or just put them in their yards.

We boys were always interested in finding the inner tubes because the rubber was excellent for slingshot use. Getting the rubber bands was the hardest part of making a slingshot. Sometimes rubber came as slow or fast rubber. Slow rubber was useless to us. We all wanted fast rubber, as it gave the rock its speed toward the target.

I made a trade with one of my cousins — my brand-new fish filleting knife that was made in Finland for the rubber bands of his old slingshot. His rubber bands were perfect and just what I needed. I explained to my mother that I needed a small piece of moose hide, three inches long and two inches wide. Did she have a piece in her sewing basket? She did.

Now that I had the pouch for my slingshot, I spent the better part of the afternoon slowly tying everything together with a long string. My slingshot was ready to be tested.

I went out searching and found four tin cans, lined them up, and carefully selected a pocketful of rocks, marble size. I stepped back and started firing the rocks. I didn't do too well at first, only managing to hit a few cans and probably by accident. But my slingshot worked perfectly, and it looked good. My friends and cousins said so. I didn't say anything but in my heart I was proud of myself.

Summertime came and it was a lazy time for going down to the brown waters of the Mackenzie River early in the morning with a crooked wooden fishing stick with string and a small hook on it to catch small white fish we called chubs. We boys took moose meat for bait and spent hours pulling fish out of the river so that we could help feed our sled dogs. Every family had six, seven, or eight dogs and they were always hungry, so we put a lot of time into this, trying to keep them fed. We all had our favourite fishing spots and we raised all kinds of heck with those fish.

We would always see the older men silently paddle by in their small hunting canoes on their way to check their nets in the blue water of Bear River. We always smiled and waved to each other. We were all fishermen.

The weather was hot and the time was slow, just like the river. So when we got tired or bored, we would make a small fire and go for a swim, even though the water was very cold. That's how I learned not to drown, a hundred miles south of the Arctic Circle.

Over time, I got really good at my target shooting and I would test myself by shooting at sticks floating on the Mackenzie River in both calm water and in waves. The long hours of practice made me good at hitting almost anything I aimed my slingshot at.

There is an old Anglican log church with a cast iron bell in my hometown that my cousins and my friends and I would shoot at, just to hear the bell sound. It made a beautiful clear sound that carried for some distance. Feeling in a mischievous mood, we would crawl and hide in the tall grass and when nobody was looking, we would shoot this bell, laugh, and then hide again, very still. There were several houses around the old church, and always someone would open their doors and look outside, this way and that way, to see who was making the bell ring, ready to give the culprits an earful. We never got caught. We always thought this was great fun and would ring the bell till late into the evening. (To all of you Tulita People reading this story, you now know I was one of those no-good kids who made the bell ring. I will now apologize for making your ears suffer.)

All of us kids would test ourselves against each other and would make up target games to see how good we were at shooting. I was not the best, but I got to be quite good. I would fire away at any stick, tin can, bottle or whatever target appeared to me without thinking twice about anything. I was a boy with a slingshot and I knew how to use it. I was on top of the world.

I HAD A favourite bird that was plain looking. It had grey and black feathers on its body, black, brown and white markings on its head, and a dark yellow beak. It was small and kind of chubby and fluffy. After the long winter I would wake up early and wait for this bird to sing. The song had a lot of feeling and emotion in it for me and it made my heart happy. Its song told me, "Summer is here and everything is okay." For me, the plain-looking bird was the best singer in the whole forest.

I remember walking on my Granny's rabbit-snaring trail one Sunday morning right after coming out of church. The sky was blue with not one cloud and the sun was hot, no wind. The forest was alive with the sounds of squirrels chattering, ravens yelling to each other, and butterflies sailing softly on the air. I had my slingshot in my back pocket and nine stones in my front pocket, looking for something to shoot at. It was then that I heard my favourite singer bird. I walked further into the bush trying to catch a glimpse of this bird. I didn't walk too far when I saw the bird on an old willow tree singing its little heart out, as happy as could be. I stopped and listened to its song, one that I've enjoyed from the earliest times that I can remember. It was beautiful.

It was then I took my slingshot from my pocket and put a stone into it. I don't know why I did this but I did. I told myself that I couldn't possibly hit anything, it was just too far but it wouldn't hurt to try. It was a very long shot.

I lifted my slingshot and took aim. My favourite singer bird did not even notice me, when I released the rock. It was then I knew immediately, *I would not miss.*

The rock sailed in slow motion as I watched it speed toward its target. I could not stop it. My heart screamed and I screamed. I saw the rock hit the bird on the head. The bird went silent and then slowly fell forward to the earth.

The whole forest went dead in silence. I dropped my slingshot, forgetting it, and ran as fast as my legs could go to the bird. I stopped and knelt down and picked up the bird. I started to cry. God was watching me. Warm blood from the bird's broken head came over my hands and I cried harder. I prayed and asked God to be with the small bird now and to take it close to His heart. Warm salty tears came from my eyes falling on the bird's head. My tears mixed with the bird's blood and I closed my eyes and put my hands close together with the bird in between and held it over my heart. It was then that my uncle's words came to me. "Never kill or harm anything for nothing..." An important lesson I had learned when he showed me how to shoot a .22 gun several years before, but I had forgotten until now, when it was too late. I looked at my favourite singer bird and kissed its beak and asked God to forgive me.

"Dear God, I am sorry for killing this bird. Please look after my friend."

It was then I wondered if this small bird had a nest full of small ones? Had I carelessly and thoughtlessly destroyed them also? To this question, to this day, I have no answer, but I do wonder what the answer would be. It is something I cannot put out of my mind.

My eyes and the front of my shirt were wet and I walked close to the riverbank where there is a clear view of the Mackenzie River. I found a spot and knelt down and dug a small hole in the green moss. I put the small bird in it and could find no words to say. All I had was my tears and sadness. I covered the bird carefully and walked away. The forest was silent.

I found my slingshot where I had dropped it. I looked at it, remembering all of the long hours I had put into making it, and then I broke it up. I took my small pocketknife and cut up the rubber and moose hide pouch and then I took the Y part in my hands and broke it in half. I angrily threw all the parts all around so they could never be back together as a slingshot and nothing could be harmed ever again from what I had made...

When I was done destroying my slingshot, I looked up again into the blue sky and said, "I am sorry."

The squirrels started to call and the birds began to sing again — softly at first. I walked by the spot where I had buried the little bird and looked one last time ... for a long, long time.

I had just turned ten years old. It was a long time before I ever touched a slingshot again and when I did, it was only to shoot at a few tin cans. I had lost my desire to hit things with rocks.

I still wake up, early in the mornings, just before the sun comes up, every spring, to wait in bed and to listen to the beautiful song of my favourite singer bird. After all of this time and this experience, I have come to love and appreciate its music even more.

In the Land of the Naʔàcho

George Blondin

When the world was new, gigantic mammals called Naʔàcho roamed the earth. There were many different kinds of these creatures. Some were birds and some were four-legged animals. Some would kill and eat human beings. Many of these animals couldn't see very well, and had to chase people by smell. Many of them were stupid. But all were dangerous.

The people were sometimes able to turn the tables, killing and eating these huge animals. This usually happened by accident. Naʔàcho would occasionally walk into a swamp and sink. Because of their great size and weight, these creatures were unable to get out, and they died there. The people would then take their meat.

But it was far more frequent for Naʔàcho to kill people. It was useless to fight these creatures because of their great size. Not only were they powerful, but they could run very fast — faster than any man.

The people often used the fact that Naʔàcho were so big to escape from them. They would run out onto thin ice, and the huge animal chasing behind would run after them. The great beast would then fall through the ice and drown. Sometimes the fleeing people would run into thick timber and the animal chasing them would get stuck between the trees. It would be forced to back out, giving the human prey time to escape.

There was once a group of people staying at a fish lake during the cold wintertime. These people wished only to live in peace. They found it hard to believe that human beings would fight wars, even to protect themselves. Most other people at that time were peaceful as well, but a few warlike bands roamed the country. If such warriors attacked them, the fishing people would not fight. They would hide under their blankets and wail, and the warriors had only to stab them where they lay.

A pair of enormous Naʔàcho birds lived near the fish lake with their young. Every morning, one or both of the fearsome birds would come to the village to scoop up luckless human beings with their long claws, and carry the victims back to their nest. The villagers didn't run away. Instead, they tried to hide in their tents. But the cruel birds would simply poke and tear at the tents with their long beaks and claws to get their victims out. As the months went by, there were fewer and fewer people left in the village.

The people didn't know what to do. They had no way to kill the birds, since bows and arrows and clubs were not enough. It seemed that the people couldn't protect themselves.

They decided to try to appease the huge birds. They offered one person from each tent in turn every morning. Some families hid their loved ones, but it did no good in the end. The big Naʔàcho birds controlled their lives.

One morning, two young strangers came to the village. The people told the men about the big birds.

"Why don't you move away or hide, instead of offering your People every day?" the strangers asked.

"We are helpless," came the answer. "Even if we run away, the birds will follow us, because they can fly. They would find us easily."

The two young men were brothers, and they were not ordinary people. They had strong medicine powers. They went off together to try to think of a way to help. "If we don't help them, these Naʔàcho birds will continue their habit and eat everyone up," they decided.

They returned to the fishing village. "We will try to kill the Naʔàcho birds for you," they told the people.

They worked all night on the frozen lake, building a huge trap for the birds. They didn't work like everyday people: they used their extraordinary powers to first pile a huge mound of tree trunks on the lake. They melted the ice to form a trench and stuck two rows of upright timbers into it. They built a covering over the timber fences to make what looked like a tunnel or hallway. They made this trap so that it had a lot of weight on top, which would fall on the birds' necks.

By morning the brothers had the trap ready. They chose two people from the village to act as bait to lure the Naʔàcho birds.

Soon, the two giant birds flew over the lake. The bait people ran into the tunnel, and the birds swooped in after them. The big trap fell on them, as planned. Then the two brothers jumped in and cut off their heads.

Everyone in the village rejoiced. "But our job is not finished yet," the brothers said.

The next morning, they went hunting for the Naʔàcho birds' young. They found the nest and killed them. Then they went back to the village and told the people that they planned to make medicine to find out more about these evil birds. They wanted to know how many of them there were in the country.

After the brothers made medicine, they reported that there were many Naʔàcho birds in the country. The creatures were useless for food, since they were much like stringy bats, mostly huge wings and little else. They were doubly dangerous because they preyed not only on humans, but on game animals as well.

Since the gigantic birds were troublemakers, and no good to anyone, the brothers decided that they would kill them all. The Elders encouraged them.

"Go ahead," they said. "It would be good for the People." The brothers made more medicine. They were able to communicate with animals, to see world problems, and to look into the future. They reported that in a short time there would be no more of the fierce birds left. They planned to exterminate them with a disease that would make them die quickly.

Soon, all the Naʔàcho birds died off. No one has ever heard of the birds bothering anyone since then, nor has anybody seen one of them. The People were so grateful and happy that they offered the brothers two young women to be their wives, and that's the end of the story of two powerful medicine brothers.

The Drums

George Blondin

THE OLD PEOPLE tell us that the Creator gave Dene medicine powers to help them survive the hardships of living. It was part of our spiritual beliefs, just as it was part of the beliefs of all Native Peoples in Canada. The Elders say our People could not have survived without this medicine.

All people did not have the same kind of powers. Some had very strong medicine, and to them a drum song was given. The song came from the Creator and was given for a special purpose.

It's known that three or four of these special people lived in every Dene group. Medicine powers were distributed fairly among the people.

Although our People had songs for fun and dancing, drum songs were different. They were for praying, healing, seeing the future, for thanksgiving, and for preaching and teaching. Drum songs came two ways — through visions, or through a person's medicine. Life was hard in the old days, and people depended on the drum for spiritual strength.

A certain man saw visions at various times in his life. Once he saw a vision of four drums. There was no one else around at the time, just this man and four drums in the air. He could hear someone singing, and knew that the song was a gift for him, a message from the Creator. The words went something like this:

> *My People, the time on this Earth is very short. Be good people, help each other. Work hard: that's part of my order. Don't complain. Love one another. Listen to the drum song and live by it.*

Many songs were passed from generation to generation. That's why we know how to sing drum songs even now, although a lot of us —especially the young — have forgotten where the songs came from and what their original purpose was. When the missionaries

Illustration: Ruth Schefter (R. Mountain)

came, people started going to church and used new ways of praying, along with the traditional songs.

In the early, early days, the Dene moved in small groups on the land, following game all year long. Every summer, the people gathered together. They would have a big drum dance, and the medicine people would sing prayer songs. They would ask the Creator for help during the coming year, and give thanks for all that had passed. They would walk slowly around in a big circle, singing and beating on the drum. The people followed in the circle, praying. As soon as they ended one song, they would start another. After prayers, the social part of the dance would begin and everyone would have a good time. That was the way they conducted a drum dance in the old days.

When the White People Came

George Blondin

ABOUT two hundred years ago, a large number of Dene lived on the bank of the Great River, Dehcho, close to the Delta. It was about the time the first white people began to wander around the country, when the Dene lifestyle was still based on medicine power.

It's hard to define medicine power: you have to have a lifetime in a medicine world to explain it, because it's so complicated. But it is useful for many things, especially if you have to investigate something or look into the future. Some individuals had strong medicine power. These medicine people used many different methods, never one the same — according to the kind of medicine they owned. This story is about a certain medicine man who chose a strange way to investigate a mystery.

The people on the banks of Dehcho lived by fishing and making dry fish. In the spring, many different kinds of fish went up the river; they would come back down in the fall. This was the circle of the seasons.

One spring day, children playing on the riverbank saw some strange chips of wood floating by. Curious, they picked them up; they had never seen woodchips like these. They took them to their parents. It was the first time the grownups had ever seen such woodchips. They were different from the ones stone axes made, and no one knew what to make of them.

"They seem like fresh chips," said the parents. "Whoever made them is up the river." There was more talk of this mystery, and it led to fear. "Maybe there are enemies coming this way," the People said. In those days, the Dene had many enemies, who often kidnapped their children.

The people knew they must do something. A strong medicine man was chosen to find out where the chips had come from.

"Let's go down to the river," said the medicine man. "I'll make my medicine there." He searched the bank and picked up a small piece of driftwood, shaped like a smoking pipe. He sat down among the people and announced, "I need something else, so I'll make more medicine. Just watch me."

The man began singing and chanting, and very shortly a mouse scampered up to him, squeaking. The medicine man talked to the mouse in mouse language. Then he stood up with the driftwood stick shaped like a smoking pipe, and put it in the water, where it floated. The medicine man squeaked to the mouse, and the mouse jumped onto the stick. When the man pronounced an ancient word and clapped his hands together, the stick with the mouse on it shot up the river like a tiny speedboat.

Everyone was amazed, but the medicine man just kept on speaking in medicine language. After about an hour, the small stick with the mouse on it came back. The medicine man and the mouse squeaked together for a long time, and then the mouse disappeared.

The medicine man spoke to the people at last. "There are strange people travelling down the river in three canoes. There are three white-skinned people with Dene guides. I have checked on their minds to see if they mean to harm our People. But they are peaceful, and are just travelling in this land. They're not far up the river, and soon they will be here."

The people went back to their tents, talking excitedly, and in the evening three canoes appeared. As they drew into shore, the People grew afraid, but the medicine man reminded them that the newcomers would not harm anyone.

This was the first time the people at the Delta had seen white men, and they greeted them the best they could, using sign language and the help of the guides. The whites gave them small presents, such as matches, pocketknives, and lump sugar. The Dene were really surprised when they struck a match and saw instant fire, but the most important thing the white men did was show them how to fire a gun.

One of the white men stuck a big stick into the ground as a target. He stepped back and loaded his gun, then aimed it and shot. The People didn't expect the loud bang, and as the gun was fired some of them yelled as if they themselves had been shot. Some ran away. Then the white man showed them the big hole the blast had made in the target, and the Dene were amazed that the gun could do that.

The white men said they would bring more of these things to trade in exchange for the fur of wild animals. In spite of the poor communication, the Dene understood what the white people were seeking when they travelled down the Great River.

Acknowledgments

Sarah Stewart

THANK YOU to Raymond Yakeleya who collected all the interviews in this book from his Elders for the documentary film, *We Remember*. Thanks to Bill Stewart for his additional research, photographs, and support. Sarah Jerome and Bella Ross for translation into Gwich'in. Sarah Look, daughter of Sarah and James Simon, added information on the Elders' biographies. Margaret Thom of the then-Slavey Research Institute who gave her full support in coordinating the translation of the manuscript into Gwich'in. Dr. Robert Janes, former Director of the Prince of Wales Northern Heritage Centre, who reviewed the original manuscript and to Margaret Bertulli: Arctic archaeologist at the Prince of Wales Northern Heritage Centre.

Thanks to the following for use of archival materials: Nick Ketchum, formerly at CBC North, Lee Selleck, formerly with the Native Communications Society, and the former Department of Information, Government of the NWT.

Thank you also to Walter Blondin, Colette Poitras, and Leanne Goose for contributing stories and essays. Leanne Goose also provided a valued Indigenous perspective on copyediting. Thanks to Ted and Violet Blondin for giving permission to reprint the stories by George Blondin, and to TouchWood Editions for allowing reprint of Antoine Mountain's story. This edition of the book is greatly enhanced by Antoine Mountain's artwork throughout, and the delicate illustrations by Ruth Schefter and Deborah Desmarais.

Thank you for financial support provided by Canada Council of two thousand dollars in 1982 for transcription and editing and also to the Government of the Northwest Territories who provided funding for the Gwich'in translation and practical support. The publisher also wishes to acknowledge support from the Alberta Media Fund and the Canada Book Fund.

Thank you to Lorene Shyba of Durvile Publications for understanding and valuing this project, and working so tirelessly to publish this important part of history.

Authors

Sarah Stewart | Raymond Yakeleya | Walter Blondin | Colette Poitras

Sarah Stewart, *Editor*

Sarah Stewart is a teacher, researcher, editor and writer. She, with Esther Tennenhouse, created the *Let's go hunting, Let's go fishing, Let's go trapping* activity books for Northern children.

Raymond Yakeleya, *Editor/Filmmaker*

Raymond Yakeleya is proud that his film, TV, and book work is used to educate future generations about the Dene People and other First Nations in a way that respects all cultures.

Walter Blondin.

Walter Blondin is a pilot, hunter, and trapper who worked his entire life in the energy industry. He loves his land and people and cares deeply for the spirituality, principals, and values of the Sahtù Dene.

Colette Poitras

Colette Poitras is Red River Métis and Chair of the Canadian Federation of Library Associations Indigenous Matters Committee. She believes libraries have a duty to preserve and revitalize Indigenous languages.

Authors

George Blondin

Leanne Goose

Antoine Mountain

George Blondin

The late George Blondin was a writer, a wilderness guide, a miner, and trapper. His books include *When the World was New* and *Yamoria, the Lawmaker.*

Leanne Goose

Leanne Goose is a singer-songwriter, musician, producer, and storyteller, born in Inuvik. She is from the Lennie/Menacho/Goose families which extend from the Arctic Coast through the Mackenzie Valley.

Antoine Mountain.

Artist, writer, and scholar Antoine Mountain is originally from *Radilih Koe/* Fort Good Hope. He is author of *From Bear Rock Mountain: The Life and Times of a Dene Residential School Survivor.*

We Remember the Coming of the White Man, Special Edition
is the fifth book in Durvile and UpRoute Book's
"Spirit of Nature" series. Series editor, Raymond Yakeleya

DURVILE & UpRoute Books

Durvile.com

Other Books in the Spirit of Nature Series

Series Editors: Raymond Yakeleya and Lorene Shyba

The Tree by the Woodpile and Other Dene Spirit of Nature Tales
Author: Raymond Yakeleya
Illustrations: Deborah Desmarais

978-1-988824-03-1 *(pbk)* | 978-1-988824-52-9 *(audiobook)*
978-1-988824-16-1 *(e-book)*

Living in the Tall Grass: Poems of Reconciliation
Author: Chief R. Stacey Laforme

978-1-988824-05-5 *(pbk)* | 978-1-988824-32-1 *(audiobook)*
978-0-968975-49-7 *(e-book)*

Lillian & Kokomis: The Spirit of Dance
Foreword: Chief R. Stacey Laforme
Author: Lynda Partridge
Illustrations: Dave Nicholson

978-1-988824-27-7 *(pbk)* | 978-1-988824-29-1 *(audiobook)*
978-1-988824-28-4 *(e-book)*

We Remember the Coming of the White Man, First Edition
Authors: Elizabeth Yakeleya, Sarah Simon *et al*
Editor: Sarah Stewart
Foreword: Raymond Yakeleya

978-1-988824-24-6 *(pbk)* | 978-1-988824-37-6 *(audiobook)*
978-1-988824-56-7 *(e-book)*

Durvile Publications gratefully acknowledges the traditional territories of the Indigenous Peoples of Southern Alberta, which includes the Siksika, Piikani, and Kainai of the Blackfoot Confederacy; the Dene Tsuut'ina; and the Chiniki, Bearspaw, and Wesley Nakoda First Nations. Also the Region III Métis Nation of Alberta.